# NINE NOBLE VIRTUES

# NINE NOBLE VIRTUES

*Cultivating the Fruit of the Spirit*

## BIBLE PORTALS
### BOOK IV

## TOM GOODMAN

MAINSAIL MEDIA

# THE "BIBLE PORTALS" BOOK SERIES

This book is part of a series called *Bible Portals: Stepping into the Pages of Scripture*. In the final pages, learn more about the series and discover other volumes in the study set.

## Endorsements

"I am excited to see the development of this new series by Tom Goodman. Bringing his commitments to Holy Scripture and his insights gained through four decades of faithful pastoral ministry, Goodman has put together thoughtful and well conceived resources to enable pastors, church staff members, and church leaders in their various teaching ministries in local congregations. These outstanding works focus on key sections of Scripture such as the Beatitudes, the Lord's Prayer, the Fruit of the Spirit, significant Psalms, and other important themes. The volumes are carefully outlined, well written, applicable, and accessible. I am happy to recommend this helpful series." —***David S. Dockery, President and Distinguished Professor of Theology, Southwestern Baptist Theological Seminary***

"Tom Goodman draws from the deep well of the Scriptures and his lifelong journey to understand and apply the wisdom of God for the regular person. He is doing it again with this new series of books called "Bible Portals." In readable, relatable chapters, you will find the insights to set a clear path for your future happiness. Enjoy!" ***Tim Hawks, Directional Team, Christ Together Network***

GET A SHOT OF INSPIRATION
IN YOUR INBOX EACH WEEK!

Subscribe to Tom's devotional newsletter, *Winning Ways*. Find it at
tomgoodman.substack.com

# INTRODUCTION

*"How long are you going to wait before
you demand the best for yourself?"*
**The Stoic philosopher, Epictetus**

While exercising, I sometimes count my reps by repeating a famous list of virtues. The Apostle Paul called it "the fruit of the Spirit."

You've probably seen this list on a poster or a plaque in a craft store: "The fruit of the Spirit is love, joy, peace, forbearance, kindness, goodness, faithfulness, humility, and self-control" (Galatians 5:22-23, CSB).

People have always relied on lists to recall the characteristics they should aspire to. As an adolescent, I repeated the Twelve Laws of Scouting every week with my Boy Scout troop. Many young men have benefited from Jordan Peterson's book, *Twelve Rules for Life*. Samurai warriors had the bushido, a code of conduct that still exerts its influence over Japanese culture today. Buddhism has the "Four Immeasurables," Confucianism taught five virtues, and Taoism has three. Benjamin Franklin managed his life under thirteen principles, and some people today gather in "Ben Franklin Circles" to practice these principles together.

Many in Western cultures have sought to structure their lives through the beliefs and practices of the Stoics. This ancient philosophy has enjoyed a small revival in our day. The Stoic philosophers taught four core and interconnected virtues: wisdom, justice, courage, and temperance.

The Apostle Paul was familiar with the Stoics, along with other Greek philosophers, poets, and playwrights. He quoted from them in his New Testament speeches and letters. Likely, he used these references to gain a hearing with his Greek and Roman audiences.

In that vein, I don't doubt that he composed his list of the "fruit of the Spirit" in light of the surrounding culture's practice of enumerating admirable qualities. As a result, we now have this divinely inspired and culturally relevant standard by which we can evaluate our spiritual progress.

I've taught Paul's fruit of the Spirit many times over the years, but I decided to do something different the last time I worked through it. Instead of defining each quality and listing some steps for practicing them, I decided to tell stories. For each of the nine virtues, I held up biblical characters who exemplified them. That's what I'll do in this book. In the stories of Moses, Isaac, Dorcas, Hosea, and others, we get to see what it looks like to live Paul's nine noble virtues.

In one of my favorite songs from the late Rich Mullins, he imagined what life would have been like for Jesus as a boy. In the chorus, Mullins sang:

> *Did they tell you stories about the saints of old*
> *Stories about their faith?*

*They say stories like that make a boy grow bold*
*Stories like that make a man walk straight.* *

I think that Mullins was on to something here. I'm sure the stories of Old Testament characters inspired the boy Jesus as he "increased in wisdom and stature, and in favor with God and with people" (Luke 2:52, CSV).

These stories of virtuous people can help you, too.

I come from a Christian teaching tradition that wants everyone to see how the stories and characters in the Old Testament foreshadow Jesus. We don't want to reduce the stories of Daniel and Jonah and David into mere lessons on how to be better people. We want to show people how each individual account fits in the overall metanarrative of God's redemptive plan.

I share that conviction, as you'll see in the chapters that follow. But when we notice characteristics we admire in these biblical characters, we should want to be like them. That's not the ultimate point of the stories, but let's not ignore this value in studying the stories, either.

The writer of the New Testament book of Hebrews offered this guidance on how we should relate to our pastors: "Consider the outcome of their way of life and imitate their faith" (Hebrews 13:7, NIV). If that's worthy advice for how to relate to our pastors, it's worthy advice for how to relate to the biblical characters our pastors discuss from the pulpit.

In *After Virtue,* the late Alasdair MacIntyre advocated for stories to convey the qualities we must practice:

---

* Rich Mullins, "Boy Like Me / Man Like You," from the 1991 album, *The World as Best as I Remember It, Volume 1.*

It is through hearing stories about wicked stepmothers, lost children, good but misguided kings, wolves that suckle twin boys, youngest sons who receive no inheritance but must make their own way in the world and eldest sons who waste their inheritance on riotous living and go into exile to live with the swine that children learn or mislearn both what a child and what a parent is, what the cast of characters may be in the drama into which they have been born and what the ways of the world are. Deprive children of stories and you leave them unscripted, anxious stutterers in their actions as in their words.[*]

So, let the biblical characters in this book inspire you to pursue virtuous living, always looking to how they point you to the One who is truer and better than them all.

---

[*]  Alasdair MacIntyre, *After Virtue: A Study in Moral Theory*, 3d ed. (University of Notre Dame Press, 2007), p. 216.

# CHAPTER 1

# AFTER THE BOYS OF SUMMER ARE GONE

*"The fruit of the Spirit is love"*

Don Henley released a Grammy-winning song that topped the Billboard charts for weeks.

It was about a young woman in a beachside town. She had turned her attention from the singer to summer tourists. But the singer refused to give up on her. "I can tell you, my love for you will still be strong," he sang, "after the boys of summer are gone."*

Would you believe that God gets himself into relationships like that? Would you believe that God expects you to love the undeserving in that same way?

That's what we discover in the astonishing story of an Old Testament prophet named Hosea.

Those of us who are pastors can tell you about our "call to

---

* "The Boys of Summer" is the first track on the 1984 album, *Building the Perfect Beast*. Lyrics by Don Henley.

ministry." We all have a story of how we felt God directing us into a life of leading and teaching his people.

But I've never known a call to ministry as odd as Hosea's.

As I mentioned in the Introduction, in each chapter of this book, I'll highlight biblical characters who exemplify each of the nine noble virtues Paul listed in Galatians 5:22-23. As Hosea lived out his call to ministry, he perfectly illustrated the first quality on Paul's list.

Love.

Here was Hosea's ministry assignment: "Then the Lord said to me, 'Go again; show *love* to a woman who is *loved* by another man and is an adulteress, just as the Lord *loves* the Israelites though they turn to other gods and *love* raisin cakes'" (Hosea 3:1, CSB, emphasis added).

God used the word "love" four times in that single sentence, but as we'll see in the unfolding story, love meant different things in each instance.

- The Israelites' love was shallow and frivolous, attracted as they were to the sweet raisin cakes of pagan worship practices.

- In juxtaposition to that superficial kind of love, God's love for his people was deep and abiding.

- In imitation of God's attitude toward Israel, Hosea was to show sacrificial, costly love to his wife.

- In sharp contrast to Hosea's love for his wife, the boyfriend didn't love her as much as the money he could get for her.

## HOSEA'S TOUGH ASSIGNMENT

Notice the word "again" in verse 1: "Then the Lord said to me, 'Go again; show love to a woman who is ... an adulteress.'"

The word "again" tells us that we've dropped into the middle of the story. At the start of the book, God told the prophet to marry Gomer, whom he called "a woman of promiscuity" (1:2-3). Scholars are divided on the meaning of this.* Was Gomer already playing the field when Hosea met and married her? Or was God speaking about how the fickle nature of this woman would inevitably come to light?

I prefer the second interpretation. In effect, God was telling Hosea, "You're going to marry someone who in time will prove to be unfaithful. Marry her anyway."

Children came along, and the paternity of two of them was ambiguous. The first boy was his, but Hosea named the second child, a girl, "Not Loved." He called the third child, a boy, "Not Mine."

By the time we get to chapter 3, Gomer has run off with one of her lovers. That is when God said to Hosea, "Go and show love to your wife again."

"So I bought her," he reported (3:2). That reveals just how far she had fallen and how her lover was now treating her. She had incurred a lot of debts, and her lover wasn't going to let her out of his sight until those were paid. (Or it may indicate a much worse situation. According to some scholars, her lover was also her pimp, passing her around to others for money.†)

---

* Duane Garrett evaluates eight options scholars have considered. Duane A. Garrett, "Hosea, Joel," *The New American Commentary*, Volume 19A (Nashville: Broadman and Holman, 1997), 44-52.

† "Our curiosity is not satisfied over the exact reason for the purchase (were these her debts? was she now a slave? perhaps a prostitute working for an owner? or was this the compensation paid to the loving 'boyfriend' of verse 1

Hosea told us he bought her "for fifteen shekels of silver and nine bushels of barley." It's a vivid image of a man scraping together all the money he had and adding precious stores of grain to the total until the boyfriend was satisfied.

Once she was bought at this great price, Hosea brought her home and reminded her, "Our love is not for sharing. We are to belong to each other exclusively" (Hosea 3:3, paraphrased).

And the children? This is so beautiful. Those whose paternity was in doubt got new names. The daughter's name was changed from "Not Loved" to "Loved." The son was no longer called "Not Mine," but "Mine" (Hosea 2:23).

## GO ... SHOW LOVE

Hosea was a prophet, and the job of a prophet is to display the character and being of God. His sacrificial love for an unfaithful wife was meant to be a real-life illustration of God's love for fickle Israel.

Surely, God does not expect the same thing from us as he did from Hosea, right?

He does. All of us who belong to Christ must display the character and being of God by showing love to those who don't deserve it.

Few people will ever betray you as terribly as Gomer betrayed Hosea. But if *Hosea* was called to mirror God's love to someone who treated him as terribly as Gomer did, you can mirror God's love to the imperfect people who disappoint you in less severe ways.

Now, if you *have* been treated as poorly as Gomer treated

---

– revealing incidentally what his love was worth?)." Derek Kidner, *The Message of Hosea* (InterVarsity, 1984), Kindle Location 555.

Hosea, restoration may not be wise in every case. After all, Jesus granted that adultery justified divorce (Matthew 5:32), and Paul recommended that a Christian who is abandoned by a non-believing spouse should regard it as a release from their marital obligations (1 Corinthians 7:15). There may be a case for abuse and addiction as biblical grounds for divorce, too, as David Instone-Brewer notes in his much-discussed books.*

But our thoughts turn too quickly to a justifiable way out of the hard work of reconciliation. Simon Peter fell into that all-too-human thinking when he asked Jesus, "Lord, how many times shall I forgive my brother or sister who sins against me? Up to seven times?" Many rabbis of the day advised that forgiving someone three times was generous enough. Peter must have felt pretty good about himself for doubling that number and adding one more for good measure. But Jesus answered, "I tell you, not seven times, but seventy-seven times" (Matthew 18:21-22, NIV).

Now, if we decide to forgive and consider reconciliation, this doesn't mean you ignore the failings you're forgiving. Hosea prophesied that Israel was going to suffer the consequences for their bad choices. There was no way around that. But the point of Hosea's prophecy was to show Israel that God would never close his heart to them. Even letting them live with the consequences of their bad choices was an act of love on his part. And he would be waiting on the other end of all that pain to welcome them back.

---

* David Instone-Brewer suggests that abuse and addiction are also biblical grounds for divorce along with adultery and abandonment. See *Divorce and Remarriage in the Bible: The Social and Literary Context* (Eerdmans, 2002), and *Divorce and Remarriage in the Church: Biblical Solutions for Pastoral Realities* (IVP USA, 2006).

## MISSION POSSIBLE

How is it possible to love the undeserving the way Hosea did? It will only happen as you reflect on God's relentless love for you and then mirror that to others.

Some people think that Hosea's message came out of what he was already experiencing. In other words, they say Hosea's thinking went something like this: "Even though my heart breaks, I find myself still loving Gomer. That must be the way God still loves Israel."

But no. Hosea saw God's love toward undeserving Israel, and he represented what he discovered about God's love in his own life and marriage.

God's words in the eleventh chapter of the book make the intensity of his love even more explicit. The ten northern tribes were sometimes called "Israel," and sometimes they were called by the name of the largest tribe, Ephraim. After a long indictment on Israel's sins and the punishment they deserved, this great cry burst from God--

"How can I give you up, Ephraim?
How can I hand you over, Israel...?
My heart is changed within me;
all my compassion is aroused" (Hosea 11:8.NIV).

This is remarkable language. Here we have God talking about his feelings. God described his inner life like the churning sea or a cauldron of roiling emotions.

Now, this is the God who made the heavens and the earth. Isaiah 40:12 says he measures the waters "in the hollow of his hand" and he marks off the heavens "with the span of his hand." He rules over the whole universe with great power. Yet you can bring this kind of God great joy, or you can break his heart.

## COSTLY LOVE

The lengths God was willing to go to win us back to himself are beautifully pictured in Hosea's actions to bring his own bride home. You recall that Hosea paid Gomer's debts. Hosea said, "I bought her for fifteen shekels of silver and nine bushels of barley" (Hosea 3:2, CSB).

Do you see what that meant? He emptied himself. The fifteen shekels weren't enough, and so, with no more cash lying around, he emptied his storehouse and brought nine bushels of barley with him, too. And by paying her debts, he freed her so she could return home with him.

In that sense, Hosea lived up to his name. His name was built on the Hebrew verb *yasha*, which means "to save."

There's another name in the Bible that's built on that verb, too. Yeshua. Jesus.

Jesus became the true and better Hosea. He sacrificed himself to ransom us. The payment was far greater than what Hosea scraped together to free Gomer. Simon Peter wrote that "you were redeemed from your empty way of life ... not with perishable things like silver or gold, but with the precious blood of Christ" (1 Peter 1:18-19, CSB).

Joseph Cardinal Ratzinger (who served as the Catholic Pope Benedict XVI) wrote, "The purely calculating will always find it absurd that for man God himself should be expended. Only the lover can understand the folly of a love to which prodigality is a law and excess alone is sufficient."*

---

* Joseph Cardinal Ratzinger, *Introduction To Christianity, 2nd Edition*, translated by J. R. Foster (San Francisco: Ignatius, 2004), 184.

What's our response to this prodigality? Since God loved us in this way, are we to respond by loving *him* with everything we've got? Of course. But when Jesus told us how to respond to God's love, he said to love *others* the way he loves us: "As I have loved you, so you must love one another. By this everyone will know that you are my disciples, if you love one another" (John 13:34-35, NIV).

## YOU ARE HOSEA—YOU ARE GOMER

Will you accept that God's love for you is as relentless as Hosea's love for undeserving Gomer? Will you rest in it and live in light of it? And then, will you go out and love others the way God loves?

In one of his poems, W.H. Auden advised that you "must love your crooked neighbour with your crooked heart."* So, let's do so. Let's take to heart that God really loves us in all our stupidity and foolishness. And then let's mirror that kind of love in all our relationships.

*"GOD, I AM GOMER AND I AM HOSEA. LIKE GOMER, HELP ME to see my sin for what it really is in your eyes: spiritual adultery. And yet, like Gomer, help me to see your relentless love for me. Help me to see the cross as your great sacrifice to pay my debts and set me free. And I know I am to be like Hosea, too. You love the undeserving, including me, and I must represent you in this life by loving the undeserving, too. Help me here, Lord. Amen."*

---

* W. H. Auden , "As I Walked Out One Evening," https://poets.org/poem/i-walked-out-one-evening, accessed 10 July 2025.

## CHAPTER 2

# SARAH SMILE

*"The fruit of the Spirit is joy"*

There's a moment in *The Shawshank Redemption* where Andy, a prisoner unjustly convicted, locks himself in a room that houses the prison's public address system. He plays a recording of a Mozart opera, sending beautiful music through the hallways and exercise yard. Prisoners and guards alike become transfixed. The narrator of the story, a prisoner named Red, recalled:

> I have no idea to this day what those two Italian ladies were singing about.... I like to think they were singing about something so beautiful it can't be expressed in words, and makes your heart ache because of it. I tell you, those voices soared higher and farther than anybody in a gray place dares to dream. It was like some beautiful bird flapped into our drab little cage and made those walls dissolve away, and for

the briefest of moments, every last man at Shawshank felt free.*

Joy is like that. It can fly into the drab little cage of any circumstance and make us feel free.

Benjamin Franklin didn't include joy among his thirteen virtues. Plato and Aristotle didn't either. (Aristotle advocated for "wittiness," but he had in mind proper social engagement, not a settled mindset.) Among the famous lists of virtues, only Paul's "fruit of the Spirit" includes joy.

"What a religion is ours," Charles Spurgeon exclaimed, "in which delight becomes a duty, in which to be happy is to be obedient to a command!"†

But joy eludes those who *disbelieve* the promises God makes and *disregard* the promises God keeps.

Sarah, Abraham's wife, had to learn this lesson. Her story reminds us that it's best not to laugh *at* God when he makes a promise, but we should surely laugh *with* God when he keeps one.

## LAUGHING AT GOD

In Genesis 18, three strangers arrived at Abraham's tent. As the story unfolds, we discover this is a visitation from God himself.

During the meal between Abraham and his guests, God announced that the son he had promised Abraham thirteen years earlier would be born within the next year.

If you know the heartbreak of infertility, you can identify

---

* Stephen King, *Rita Hayworth and Shawshank Redemption* (1982).
† Charles Haddon Spurgeon, "A Harp of Ten Strings," a sermon delivered August 30, 1891. https://www.spurgeon.org/resource-library/sermons/a-harp-of-ten-strings/#flipbook/, accessed 15 June 2025.

with this couple's desire for a child. But there's more to this story than God simply giving a child to a childless couple.

When God first spoke to Abraham, he promised him, "I will make you into a great nation" (Genesis 12:2). The Messiah was to come from this nation, and thus the whole world would be blessed through Abraham's family.

But it's hard to start a nation without children, and no child came for thirteen years after the promise. Then God appeared at Abraham's tent in the guise of a stranger to tell the old man that the fulfillment of that promise was imminent.

Sarah did not react with reverent astonishment at the wonderful news:

> Then the Lord said, "I will surely return to you about this time next year, and Sarah your wife will have a son." Now Sarah was listening at the entrance to the tent, which was behind him. Abraham and Sarah were already old and well advanced in years, and Sarah was past the age of childbearing. So Sarah laughed to herself as she thought, "After I am worn out and my master is old, will I now have this pleasure?" Then the Lord said to Abraham, "Why did Sarah laugh and say, 'Will I really have a child, now that I am old?' Is anything too hard for the Lord? I will return to you at the appointed time next year and Sarah will have a son." Sarah was afraid, so she lied and said, "I did not laugh." But he said, "Yes, you did laugh." (Genesis 18:10-15, NIV.)

Some Bible teachers are charitable to Sarah. After all, they say, when she laughed, Sarah did not yet know it was the Lord who was speaking. As far as she knew, the visitors were simply travelers pronouncing a kind blessing upon a man who had fed them lunch—something like, "May your wife finally have the child you have desired all these years."

But that's too generous an interpretation. Sarah had known about God's promise of a son for over a decade. When this stranger outside her tent said she would have a son within the year, she laughed because she had given up on God a long time ago.

Notice that God forced Sarah to face her unbelief. She had laughed to herself, inside the tent. But the Lord knows our hearts, and he knew Sarah's disbelief. The Lord asked, "Why did you laugh, Sarah?"

Sarah denied her laughter, but God's response hung like a banner over the entire scene: "No, Sarah, you did laugh."

Too often, we react to God's word like Sarah did. You might think, "Me? I've never laughed at God or his word!" But give it some thought.

The Lord promises to free us from our addictions and sins, and we say, "I have been locked into these choices for too long. It's too late for me." What are we doing? We're laughing at the word of God.

God says he will wipe our entire record free of guilt, but we say, "How can the things I've done all go away simply because Jesus was nailed to a bloody cross?" When we think like that, what are we doing? We're laughing at the word of God.

Our Lord says that the bodies we plant at death will be raised into an immortal body on the last day, and we say, "Nothing in my physics class or my chemistry textbook says that such a thing is possible." When we think like that, what are we doing? We're laughing at the word of God.

There's nothing neutral about disbelieving God's word. When we disbelieve God, it's personal to him. It's as if we've reacted with dubious, cynical, mocking cackles.

And our faithless reaction may be known to no one else. We're like Sarah inside the tent, secretly living in disbelief. But God discerns it, just as he did with Sarah.

## LAUGHING WITH GOD

Genesis 18 is not the only record of Sarah's laughter, though. We see her laughing again in the opening verses of Genesis 21. Three times we're told God came through just as he said he would:

> "Now the Lord was gracious to Sarah *as he had said*, and the Lord did for Sarah *what he had promised*. Sarah became pregnant and bore a son to Abraham in his old age, *at the very time God had promised him*. Abraham gave the name Isaac to the son Sarah bore him.... Sarah said, "God has brought me laughter, and everyone who hears about this will laugh with me." (Genesis 21:1-6, NIV. Emphasis added.)

Sarah had previously laughed in cynical amusement; now she laughs with joyous amazement.

The name of their son preserved the moment. Sarah named him Isaac.

Do you know what the word "Isaac" means in Hebrew? Let me explain it this way. An adult son got a text from his mother one day. It read, "Your aunt passed away. LOL."

He was baffled. He wrote back, "Why is that funny?"

His mom replied, "What do you mean? It's certainly not funny."

He typed, "Mom, LOL means 'Laughing Out Loud'."

"Oh no!" she texted him, "I sent that to everyone! I thought it meant 'Lots of Love'!"

In Hebrew, the name "Issac" means "LOL!" Sarah said she

wanted to call him Issac because "God has brought me *laughter*."

Can you imagine it? As the infant grew into a boy, every evening she would step out of the tent and call out, "Come home, Laughter! It's time for supper!"

And every time she used his name, she would be reminded of the time she laughed *at* God when he promised a son, and the time she laughed *with* God when he gave her a son.

What a shame that we laugh when we should not, but what a shame that we do not laugh when we should!

We are to be like those Jewish pilgrims who sang in Psalm 126 (NIV), "Our mouths were filled with laughter, our tongues with songs of joy."

In his commentary on Psalm 126, the late pastor Eugene Peterson said:

> Laughter is the delight that things are working together for good to them that love God.... The joy that develops in the Christian way of discipleship is an overflow of spirit that comes from feeling good not about yourself but about God. We find that his ways are dependable, his promises sure. This joy is not dependent on our good luck in escaping hardship. It is not dependent on our good health and avoiding pain. Christian joy is actual in the midst of pain, suffering, loneliness, and misfortune. *

The Apostle Paul bore witness to this kind of joy. We love to quote his command: "Rejoice in the Lord always. I will say it again: Rejoice!" (Philippians 4:4, NIV.) But we often forget

---

* Eugene Peterson, *A Long Obedience in the Same Direction: Discipleship in an Instant Society* (Downers Grove: Intervarsity, 1980), 96-97.

that when he wrote that, he was in a prison cell. He didn't let his circumstances determine his attitude.

It wasn't that he maintained joy *despite* his conditions. He went so far as to say that his conditions *generated* his joy:

> "We rejoice in our sufferings, knowing that suffering produces endurance, and endurance produces character and character produces hope, and hope does not disappoint us, because God's love has been poured into our hearts through the Holy Spirit who has been given to us.... We also rejoice in God through our Lord Jesus Christ, through whom we have now received reconciliation" (Romans 5:3-5, 11, ESV).

Our joy cannot be based on what kind of circumstances we're in. It has to be based on the God who's walking us through those circumstances.

Sarah said it: "God has brought me laughter."

Paul said it: "God has brought me laughter."

Others I've known have said it.

As I write this chapter, I'm thinking of a woman I know who waited for decades until God answered her prayer and gave her a wonderful Christian husband. She could say it: "God has brought me laughter."

I'm thinking of a man set free from alcohol addiction. He could say it: "God has brought me laughter."

I'm thinking of a high school student living free from guilt and self-hatred. He could say it: "God has brought me laughter."

I'm thinking of a man who thought the end of his job meant the end of usefulness but now he knows otherwise. He could say it: "God has brought me laughter."

I'm thinking of a man I remember from my first church out of seminary. In the last weeks of Bob's life, before malignant melanoma took him, he would try to speak, but the cancer and the chemo had scrambled parts of his memory, so finding the words became difficult.

As I would visit with him in the hospital or at his home or in the hallway at church, he would try to express the serenity that God had given him about death. Fumbling with the thin veil that separates this life from the next, Bob would catch a glimpse of eternity. But when he tried to explain it to any of us, the words would not come. Then he would simply smile, his bright eyes fixed on a world none of us could yet see.

His smile conveyed more than words ever could. Like Sarah, Bob was silently saying, "God has brought me laughter."

Do you laugh with God? The musician Carolyn Arends wrote:

> Recently, I threw out three boxes worth of my kids' Sunday school crafts. I felt heartless and vaguely evil. But really, one can only store so much Fun Foam in a single house.
>
> Still, there was one piece of art I was compelled to save. My daughter had cut out and colored pictures of children engaged in different acts of worship, and glued them onto a sheet. (She was three; you were expecting decoupage?)
>
> Bethany had been particularly proud of this assignment because of the gluing part. (I think she may have a future in adhesives.) The day she brought it home, I acknowledged the excellence of the glue-work and then asked her to tell me about what the pictures represented. "Praying! Giving! Reading the Bible!" she shouted as I pointed to each scene.
>
> I saved the best picture for last—a boy with his mouth open wide in song. Singing is my favorite form of worship. I knew it would be Bethany's too, what with her mother being a singer and all.

"Laughing," said Bethany, when I pointed to the boy with the open mouth.

I stood corrected. Laughing is my favorite form of worship.*

Laughing is worship! In Psalm 92:4 (NIV), the poet said, "For you make me glad by your deeds, Lord; I sing for joy at what your hands have done."

In the article, Arends calls laughter "carbonated holiness." Don't you like that? When was the last time you uncorked a little of that carbonated holiness?

## "FOR THE JOY SET BEFORE HIM, HE ENDURED"

We ought not to laugh in amusement at God, but we ought to laugh in amazement with God.

Too often, we fail on both counts. We disbelieve the promises God makes, and we disregard the promises God keeps!

If we live defeated Christian lives, it is because we are both faithless and joyless: faithless as to what God says he will do and joyless as to what God does.

Jesus was—and is—the supreme example of this joy we've been talking about. In Hebrews 12:2 (NIV), we read, "For the joy set before him he endured the cross, scorning its shame, and sat down at the right hand of the throne of God."

It was for *joy* that he endured the agonies of crucifixion. The joy of pleasing his Father was enough. The joy of bringing us to the Father as his redeemed ones was enough. He gathers

---

* Carolyn Arends, "Carbonated Holiness," *Christianity Today*, March 2008, https://www.christianitytoday.com/2008/04/carbonated-holiness/, accessed 16 June 2025.

us up in a big embrace like Sarah did with her son, and he delights in us (Psalm 18:19).

And if we follow him, we'll go about life in the same way. The Christian message is, "Be like Jesus. For the joy set before him, he endured, so for the joy set before *you*, do the same!"


"GOD, FORGIVE ME FOR THE TIMES I'VE CONSIDERED YOUR *promises and responded in cynical disbelief. But I also ask your forgiveness for all the times I've failed to respond with delight to your many blessings. Free me from these failures that keep me from having the confident joy you intend for me. Amen.*"

# CHAPTER 3

# MAY THE FOURTH BE
# WITH YOU

*"The fruit of the Spirit is peace"*

In his book, *The Anxious Generation*, social psychologist Jonathan Haidt said we are "overprotecting our children in the real world while underprotecting them online."* The consequence is a widespread mental health crisis among teenagers and young adults. He says that huge numbers enter adulthood with two convictions: *The world is scary, and I don't have what it takes to navigate it.*

When hard times come, will we respond with panic or peace? Paul included peace as a fruit of the Spirit.

Let's look at three men who bore this fruit. They responded to their greatest trial with peace instead of panic because they knew God was with them. As Hebrew exiles in

---

* Quoted in James R. Wood, "A deep need for parental discretion," *World*, April 30, 2025, https://wng.org/opinions/a-deep-need-for-parental-discretion-1745975527, accessed 15 June 2025, reviewing Jonathan Haidt, *The Anxious Generation: How the Great Rewiring of Childhood Is Causing an Epidemic of Mental Illness* (New York: Penguin Press, 2024).

Babylon, they were known as Shadrach, Meshach, and Abednego.

In the third chapter of the book of Daniel, the Babylonian king set up a 90-foot-tall statue—a symbol of Babylon, of his rule over Babylon, and of the gods who made his rule possible. He ordered that all citizens and exiles pay homage to that statue and what it symbolized. These three young Hebrew men refused, even when they were threatened with a fiery death:

> Nebuchadnezzar said to them, "Is it true, Shadrach, Meshach and Abednego, that you do not serve my gods or worship the image of gold I have set up...? If you do not worship it, you will be thrown immediately into a blazing furnace. Then what god will be able to rescue you from my hand?" [They] replied to him, "King Nebuchadnezzar, we do not need to defend ourselves before you in this matter. If we are thrown into the blazing furnace, the God we serve is able to deliver us from it, and he will deliver us from Your Majesty's hand. But even if he does not, we want you to know, Your Majesty, that we will not serve your gods or worship the image of gold you have set up." Then Nebuchad-nezzar was furious..., and commanded some of the strongest soldiers in his army to tie up Shadrach, Meshach and Abed-nego and throw them into the blazing furnace (Daniel 3:14-20, NIV).

## YOUR TRIAL BY FIRE IS COMING

We use the phrase "trial by fire" to describe circumstances that test our character and resilience.

The phrase comes from European medieval practices to determine someone's guilt or innocence. The judgment was made by putting the accused through ordeals like walking over hot coals or holding a heated iron. If they endured, they were innocent; if they failed, they were guilty. The trial by fire proved it.

The Babylonian king put these three young believers through a *judgment* by fire, not a trial. He threatened them with a fiery death and then sentenced them to it.

But it proved to be a trial by fire after all. The whole experience was a trial that proved the resilience of their faith and their trust in God's presence.

Your trial by fire is coming. It may be some heartbreak over one of your children, or a betrayal by a marriage partner, or a pink slip at work, or a doctor's report that changes your entire world.

Whatever it will be, are you ready?

Even Christians surrounded by this increasingly secular culture are surprised to find how unprepared they are when suffering comes. Adrian Warnock wrote:

> At age 46, my life as I knew it was interrupted without warning. Like countless days before, I was commuting home from a normal day in the office. Suddenly I found myself at a train station struggling to walk or even breathe. An ambulance took me off to the hospital, where I was told I had pneumonia. But then a blood test revealed an abnormality, which resulted in a more sinister diagnosis: a slow-growing form of leukemia....
>
> I am a medical doctor and have also received a lot of sound biblical teaching. So you'd think I would have been ready when suffering hit. But I was surprised at what a blow it was. In retrospect, I can see more clearly why.
>
> First, I see that the blessings of my society shaped my expectations. Like most who read this article, I live in a

historical anomaly when it comes to suffering. I have access to clean water, sanitary food, amazing medical technologies, rapid emergency-response systems, and social welfare support if I'm unable to work. As a result, I am protected from so many dangers that afflicted my ancestors, and I can feel like everything is under my own control. I can see now how much I assumed I'd be spared from suffering.

Second, I was unprepared because to some extent I had absorbed a faulty functional theology that many of us share in the Western church today. It isn't the theology I've been taught or thought I believed. But somehow I had not sufficiently challenged the assumption that if I worship and serve God faithfully, he would shield me from serious suffering.*

## GOD'S PRESENCE AND GOD'S RESCUE

How can you respond to tough times with peace instead of panic? By *trusting in God's presence* and *waiting for God's rescue*.

God was present with these three young Hebrew men in a dramatic way. Shortly after they were thrown into the furnace, the king "leaped to his feet in amazement" and asked his advisers, "Weren't there three men that we tied up and threw into the fire?" When they confirmed it, he said, "Look! I see four men walking around in the fire, unbound and unharmed, and the fourth looks like a son of the gods" (Daniel 3:24-25, NIV).

Of course, reading this story from the perspective of the New Testament, we know who this fourth being was: not a son of the gods but the Son of God, the pre-incarnate Christ present with his people when they needed him most.

---

* Adrian Warnock, "Surprised by Trials," *Desiring God*, July 17, 2018, https://www.desiringgod.org/articles/surprised-by-trials, accessed 15 June 2025.

The rescue was just as dramatic. The king ordered them to come out of the fire, and when all the royal officials "crowded around them," they saw that "the fire had not harmed their bodies, nor was a hair of their heads singed; their robes were not scorched, and there was no smell of fire on them" (Daniel 3:26-27, NIV).

Does God really rescue his people like that? Yes.

Always? Yes.

We're rescued in this life or eternity, but he always rescues.

When he rescues us in this life, rejoice. When the physical healing inexplicably comes and baffles the doctors, when money shows up unexpectedly to enable us to keep a roof over our heads, when the job opportunity shows up when no one seemed to be hiring—thank God for those moments.

But he always rescues—if not in this life, then in eternity.

In the Book of Revelation, the Apostle John told us what he saw in heaven:

> I looked, and there before me was a great multitude that no one could count, from every nation, tribe, people and language, standing before the throne and before the Lamb. They were wearing white robes and were holding palm branches in their hands.... These are they who have come out of the great tribulation....
> They are before the throne of God
>     and serve him day and night in his temple;
> and he who sits on the throne
>     will shelter them with his presence.
> Never again will they hunger;
>     never again will they thirst.
> The sun will not beat down on them,'
>     nor *any scorching heat*" (Revelation 7:9-16, NIV).

There's only one right word to describe that scene: *rescued*. The countless martyrs whom John saw had faced their own fiery furnace, and they were rescued—not in this life but in eternity.

Now, some may think, "That's not the kind of rescue I want! What good is this religion you teach if it doesn't promise to save my marriage or cure my cancer or get my rent covered?"

But this line of thinking just reveals that, to you, God is simply a means to an end. He is an instrument you use to get what you think you really need. You don't think you need *him*; you just need the stuff you hope he'll provide.

I go to a loan officer at a bank not to build a relationship with the banker but to get a loan. The banker is only useful to me if I get that loan. That's the way some of us relate to God. And if we don't get our crisis solved on our terms, in this earthly life, what good is God to us?

## NAIL-SCARRED FEET

God always accompanies his people in our trials. This was beautifully illustrated in the animated short film, *The 21.*\* It's about the twenty-one Christians beheaded by ISIS terrorists on a Libyan beach in 2015. The animation is hand-drawn by 70 artists from more than 24 countries in the style of Coptic icons. It was short-listed for a 2024 Oscar.

It's sad and inspiring and beautiful.

One of the striking things about the film is discovering who accompanies these martyrs to their execution. Jesus appears among the men throughout the film—in one particu-

---

\* Learn more about the film at https://www.the21film.com. Watch the 13-minute film at https://youtu.be/XwPQqkeeCTg, accessed 15 June 2025.

larly moving scene, one martyr steps into the place on the beach for his execution, and then another pair of nail-scarred feet steps into the frame.

Just as God joined Shadrack, Meshack, and Abednego in the fire until they were rescued in this earthly life, he joined the 21 martyrs on the Libyan beach in their fiery furnace until they were rescued in eternal life. The moment they were beheaded, Revelation 7 says they stood before the throne of God in white robes holding palm branches in their hands, and he who sits on the throne shelters them with his presence.

What does it mean for the feet of Jesus to bear nail scars?

It means he faced his own fiery furnace. He suffered and died on the cross. And there he took care of the sin problem that separated us from him.

The night before Jesus went to the cross, he told his disciples, "I have told you these things, so that in me you may have peace. In this world you will have trouble. But take heart! I have overcome the world" (John 16:33, NIV).

There's that word again: peace. In this world, you will have trouble, but you can face it with peace instead of panic.

How? You get this peace he promises through humility and patience.

## HUMILITY AND PATIENCE

First, you have to receive it humbly. In John 16:33, notice the words "in me." Jesus said, "I have told you these things, so that *in me* you may have peace" (emphasis added).

The kind of peace that transcends circumstances is not the kind that you work up within yourself or accomplish on your own. Jesus provides it.

He said, "I have overcome the world." What does that mean? He was talking about all that he accomplished for us by coming into our world, dying in our place on the cross, rising in victorious resurrection, and ascending back to heaven until he comes again to set everything right. He summarizes it all by speaking in the past tense: "I have overcome the world." It was so assured that he could speak of it all as if it were already accomplished.

So, peace isn't something we develop inside us—he provides it. And we have to humbly ask him for this resource.

Am I promising that once you begin a relationship with Christ you'll go through life never anxious over anything ever again?

No. I said you need to receive the peace of Christ humbly *and patiently*. What I mean is, peace doesn't come overnight.

Now, there are certainly moments when it floods your soul. But if you want a settled and immovable sense that God is working all things together for our good, that only comes over time.

In John 16:33, when Jesus said, "I have told you *these things* so that in me you may have peace," he was referring to all he had taught them. Things about his death and resurrection and return, things about the abiding presence of the Holy Spirit and how to get along with each other. And now he said, "Here's why I told you all this: So that you might have peace."

What does that mean? We have peace only as we reflect on those words and apply those words to what we experience as we go through life. And that takes time.

If you hear an accomplished guitarist and it inspires you to give the instrument a try, just buying a guitar doesn't mean you'll be playing great music by next week.

Becoming a Christian is a big step toward real peace. But it takes time to live in that reality and *act* from that reality. How's your guitar practice going? What Jesus taught us about

God and life is like notes on sheet music. We have to practice the gospel—rehearse it, mull over it, meditate on it.

## THE HARVEST OF PEACE

Jesus said, "The Holy Spirit, whom the Father will send in my name, will teach you all things and will remind you of everything I have said to you. Peace I leave with you; my peace I give you. I do not give to you as the world gives. Do not let your hearts be troubled and do not be afraid" (John 14:26-27, NIV).

So, when the Holy Spirit reminds us of the way Jesus said we should think and behave, we'll have peace. That's why Paul called peace the fruit of the Spirit.

This means that peace is the product or the end result of letting God reign in your life. When we use phrases like "the fruit of our labors" or "a fruitful effort," we're speaking about the result of something. So, when Paul said peace was a fruit of the Spirit, he meant that peace is the result of the Spirit of God at work.

When we study his word and trust it, when we teach and sing about his word and believe it, the fruit of all that is peace. Even in our heartbreaks and hard times, there is a flowing undercurrent of confidence that God is working to fulfill his promises to us.

The Babylonian king was startled to see that the three men he had condemned to death had company: "Look! I see *four* men walking around in the fire, unbound and unharmed, and the *fourth* looks like a son of the gods." (Daniel 3:24-25, NIV. Emphasis added.)

Four men.

My social media feeds blow up with *Star Wars* memes on May the Fourth every year. That's because the date sounds similar to the most famous line in the films: "May the Force be with you."

I like *Star Wars*. (Well, I like the first three movies of the franchise.) But I'm hoping you'll remember another story on that day every year: the story of Shadrach, Meshach, and Abednego in the fiery furnace.

Whatever you're going through, may the Fourth be with you.

*"JESUS, I WANT TO RESPOND TO MY TRIALS WITH PEACE INSTEAD of panic. You graciously offer peace to me, and I receive it humbly and patiently. I receive it humbly, putting my trust in you. And I commit to patience: I commit to practicing the gospel like someone practices music until it becomes my life. Amen."*

# CHAPTER 4

# DIG ANOTHER WELL

*"The fruit of the Spirit is forbearance"*

We now come to what I call the "and so forth" part of Paul's list. When people refer to this famous passage, they often say, "The fruit of the Spirit is love, joy, peace, and so forth." So, in this chapter, we'll begin the "and so forth" section of the list.

A lot of our translations use the word "patience" here, and some of our translations use the word "longsuffering." The New Life Version translates it as "not giving up." All those words and phrases convey the same idea. The New Testament was written in Greek, and the Greek word here means to *hold up* or *withstand*.

The Ancient Greeks used the word to speak of a fence that was strong enough to withstand the pressure of livestock leaning against it. They used the word to describe a tree on a tall cliff that held up against relentless winds.

A young man named Isaac is a good illustration of this quality. He had a huge flock of sheep and goats, and he needed to ensure that his animals had enough water. But his enemies stopped up his wells, filling them with dirt. In Genesis 26, we find out how Isaac reacted to this:

> So Isaac moved away from there and encamped in the Valley of Gerar and settled there. Isaac reopened the wells that had been dug in the time of his father Abraham, which the Philistines had stopped up after Abraham died, and he gave them the same names his father had given them. Isaac's servants dug in the valley and discovered a well of fresh water there. But the herdsmen of Gerar quarreled with Isaac's herdsmen and said, "The water is ours!" So he named the well Esek [meaning *dispute*], because they disputed with him. Then they dug another well, but they quarreled over that one also; so he named in Sitnah [meaning *opposition*]. He moved on from there and dug another well, and no one quarreled over it. He named it Rehoboth [meaning *room*], saying, "Now the LORD has given us room and we will flourish in the land" (Genesis 26:17-22, NIV).

Maybe things aren't going your way right now. Circumstances or people have interrupted your plans. When things don't go your way, you have to fight two temptations—blowing up and giving up. Either you want to lash out at the people who are making life difficult for you, or you want to quit trying.

When you have forbearance like Isaac, you won't *blow up* or *give up* when things don't go your way.

## DON'T BLOW UP

Isaac could have lashed out at his Philistine enemies. I mean, every well that was mentioned in this story was rightfully his.

Instead, he moved on, going a little farther out and a little farther away each time, until finally everyone was satisfied.

Why did he do that? Even though he was powerful, if he fought his Philistine neighbors, they could have banded together and overwhelmed him.

Sometimes, trying to even things up hurts you more than it hurts your enemy.

Maybe you read the strange story of a man in South Carolina who threatened another man with a deadly weapon: a cottonmouth water moccasin. The man using the snake against his intended victim was the one who got bitten.[*]

Then there's the story about a 36-year-old man in Oregon who suffered a self-inflicted gunshot wound. He had been trying to shoot a squirrel with his .22 rifle. As he drew a bead on the animal, it suddenly ran up his leg. When he pulled the trigger, he shot himself in the foot.[†]

Anger and bitterness can make you the object of an offbeat news item. Or it can result in consequences much worse.

Are there times we need to stand our ground instead of yielding to the enemy? Sure. Sometimes we'll need to file a formal complaint, or involve the authorities, or get a lawyer. But, too often, these stands are more about our ego and our control than anything else.

When things didn't go Isaac's way, he could have blown up. But it would have destroyed him, and it would have hurt those he was responsible for. So, he kept his attention on the

---

[*] "Four arrested for threatening man with poisonous snake," WIS-TV, Jun. 16, 2007, https://www.wistv.com/story/6643184/four-arrested-for-threatening-man-with-poisonous-snake/, accessed 22 June 2025.

[†] Randy Cassingham, "Ready, Fire, Aim!" *This is True*, December 18, 2011. http://www.thisistrue.com.

most urgent issue: his flocks needed water. So, he kept digging wells.

We'll need the kind of forbearance Isaac demonstrated when people oppose us. But we'll need it just as much when family members or colleagues simply annoy us.

In the book of Proverbs, the wise man wrote, "Disregarding another person's faults preserves love" (Proverbs 17:9, NLT). In Proverbs 19:11 (CSB), we read, "A person's insight gives him patience, and his virtue is to overlook an offense."

In none of those passages does the writer refer to enemies. If God expects us to forbear enemies who oppose us, he certainly expects us to put up with colleagues who annoy us.

Healthy relationships can only develop when people are committed to this quality of patience and forbearance. "Be completely humble and gentle," Paul wrote, adding "be patient, bearing with one another in love" (Ephesians 4:2, NIV).

How can you increase your capacity for forbearance? Pay attention to four things.

**Personality**. Some are introverts, others are extroverts. In making decisions, some are methodical and others are spontaneous. Not everyone thinks like us, reacts like us, or communicates like us. The more we are sensitive to this, the better we can forbear annoyances.

**Perspective**. As the old saying goes, "Don't judge a man until you've walked a mile in his shoes." The old proverb advises us to see things as others see them. In that way, we become more understanding of others.

**Progress**. We can be more patient with people if we consider where they are in their physical, emotional, and spiritual progress. For example, parents of small children can get so impatient when they forget what a challenge it is for a little one to tie his shoelaces or get the zipper started on his jacket.

If we'll keep in mind that people are at different stages than we are physically, emotionally, and spiritually, it will help us bear irritations in relationships.

***Problems***. Someone else's behavior may spring from the stuff they're dealing with. Their parents' divorce. Their husband's Alzheimer's disease. Their adult child's poor choices. Their shame, fears, and regrets. The more we know that, and the more we take it into account, the more we can bear with other people.

## DON'T GIVE UP

When faced with hard times, those who don't blow up might give up. We decide it's not worth the effort anymore.

Blowing up and giving up are both destructive, but blowing up is what you do to other people, while giving up is what you do to yourself.

Isaac could have thrown up his hands in defeat. His enemies covered up every well his father dug, and they caved in every new well Isasc dug. But he said to himself, "I will never stop trying, and I will never try stopping."

It may be that your hardships are not tempting you to blow up but to give up. If so, let me tell you about a pilot named Henry Dempsey.

On a commuter flight from Portland, Maine, to Boston, Dempsey heard an unusual noise near the rear of the small aircraft. He turned the controls over to his co-pilot and went back to check it out.

As he reached the tail section, the plane hit an air pocket, which tossed Dempsey against the rear door. He quickly discovered the source of the mysterious noise. The rear door had not been properly latched before takeoff, and it flew open. He was instantly sucked out of the jet.

When the co-pilot saw the red light indicating an open door, he radioed the nearest airport. He requested permission to make an emergency landing and requested an ocean search for Dempsey.

After the plane landed, they found Henry Dempsey. He was not in the ocean. He was clinging to the outdoor ladder of the aircraft. Somehow, he had caught the ladder and held on for ten minutes as the plane flew 200 miles per hour at an altitude of four thousand feet. It took airport personnel several minutes to pry Dempsey's fingers from the ladder!*

I imagine that any time Dempsey felt like giving up his grip on that ladder, he just looked down and considered the alternative.

Forbearance isn't just for dealing with enemies who threaten you or colleagues who annoy you. You need it if you're overcoming addiction, recovering from failure, or achieving that goal you know God wants you to reach for.

Paul wrote to Timothy and, by extension, all of us who pastor, "Preach the word ... with great *patience....* *Keep your head* in all situations, *endure* hardship..., *discharge* all the duties of your ministry" (2 Timothy 4:2-5, NIV).

It's a quality all of us need in any area of service, not just pastors. Paul wrote to *all* Christians when he said, "Let us *not become weary* in doing good, for at the proper time we will reap a harvest *if we do not give up*" (Galatians 6:9, NIV. Emphasis added).

I read about a Seattle businessperson, Don Bennett, who achieved one of his lifelong dreams to climb Mount Rainier. Getting to the top of that mountain would be impressive

---

* "Pilot, Sucked Out of Plane, Hangs Tight Till Landing," Los Angeles *Times*, September 3, 1987. https://www.latimes.com/archives/la-xpm-1987-09-03-mn-5933-story.html, accessed 22 June 2025.

enough, but Bennett did it on one leg. He was the first amputee to scale that 14,410-foot mountain. It took him five days.

When asked how he did it, Bennett said, "One hop at a time."*

That's how you withstand difficult people and difficult circumstances. You'll only advance if you take it one hop at a time.

## "A SPRING OF WATER WELLING UP"

Now, how do we develop this forbearance that keeps us from blowing up or giving up?

When I was a Boy Scout, we recited the Boy Scout Law at every meeting: "A Scout is trustworthy, loyal, helpful, friendly, courteous, kind, obedient, cheerful, thrifty, brave, clean, and reverent." For a middle school boy, it was a helpful list of qualities to aspire to.

Should we see Paul's list of the fruit of the Spirit in the same way?

Well, on the one hand, it would take you a long way toward living a better life if you did. Imagine if everyone you knew committed to living a life of love, joy, peace, and patience—just to name the first four qualities we've looked at in this series.

But it's important to note that Paul called all these things "the fruit of the Spirit." The qualities Paul listed are the *results* of letting the Spirit work in your life. Learn from God, trust

---

* James M. Kouzes and Barry C. Posner, *The Leadership Challenge*: *How to Make Extraordinary Things Happen in Organizations* (San Francisco: Jossey-Bass, 1987), 217.

God, let God work in you, and you'll notice these qualities showing up more and more.

Once more, Isaac is our model here. As we've seen, Isaac did not blow up or give up. But why?

Because he had a deep trust in God.

We see this by how he named his wells. He named the first one "Esek," meaning "Dispute." He named the second one "Sitnah," meaning "Opposition." But he named the third one "Rehoboth," meaning "Room." Why? Isaac said, "Now the Lord has given us room and we will flourish in the land" (Genesis 26:22, NIV).

When things didn't go his way, Isaac decided, "God blessed me once and he can do it again."* That's how forbearance showed up in his life. He got his eyes off the problem and lifted them to the God who had the solution.

There's another story about a well in the New Testament. Just as experiences with wells taught Isaac to trust God, Jesus once used a well to teach a woman about trust. On the outskirts of a Samaritan village, Jesus sat beside a well to rest. A woman came from the village to draw water, and they got to talking. Jesus told her, "Everyone who drinks this water will be thirsty again, but whoever drinks the water I give them will never thirst. Indeed, the water I give them will become in them a spring of water welling up to eternal life" (John 4:13-14, NIV).

He was promising her and, by extension, all of us, that if

---

* This line comes from Paul Overstreet, "Dig Another Well," from the album, *Sowin' Love*, 1989. The album produced five top-10 singles for Overstreet. One of my favorite memories from my days of serving as a pastor in the Cayman Islands was a small dinner party that included Paul and his wife, Julie, who were visiting the island. The hostess asked Paul to play some of his hit songs, which he graciously agreed to do.

we give ourselves to him and let him be the Savior and Lord of our lives, we'll find all we need to make it through life.

Isaac exemplified perseverance by neither losing control nor abandoning hope. The Spirit of Jesus cultivates this steadfastness in those who surrender to his transformative influence in their lives.

*"Lord Jesus, give me living water from your well that never runs dry. I commit to you as my Savior and Lord. I turn life's setbacks over to you right now. Help me not to blow up or give up. Help me to know that you are not simply the God of the good old days. You are the God of good new days, too. You've blessed me before, and you can do it again!"*

# CHAPTER 5

# CULTIVATING KINDNESS

*"The fruit of the Spirit is kindness"*

"The scissors snipped together slowly making that unmistakable crunching sound, and 10 inches of hair that I spent two years growing were gone."

But Rebecca Harrington wasn't in the salon for a new look. The clipped hair was going to an organization that creates wigs for children and young adults diagnosed with alopecia or who've lost their hair during chemotherapy.

Sufferers appreciate the gift. Jessica Melore described the daily process of losing her hair as "an outward manifestation of being sick." Each day, she found more strands in the drain when she took a shower or on her pillow when she woke up. "It's a little bit of sadness like, 'Oh there it goes, I'm on my way to being bald,'" she said. Getting a wig was an important boost for her well-being.

One wigmaker described how girls with alopecia go "from sad, lowered faces to smiling, hair-flipping girls" because of the donated hairpieces.

When eight-year-old Brandi Gamache decided to donate fourteen inches of her long, strawberry-blond hair, it was a big step. Brandi had fought for years to keep her hair long, despite her mom's complaints about how difficult it was to manage.

Then she read a book about a girl going through chemotherapy and decided to take the step. The stylist "told me to close my eyes," Brandi said. "And when I opened them up it was like...." To complete the sentence, she opened her eyes wide in astonishment. But she was pleased that another little girl would benefit from her donation.[*]

The biblical writers would call this an act of *kindness*. We tend to think of kindness as mere inoffensiveness. But when Paul called kindness a fruit of the Spirit, he wasn't talking about good manners.

Of course, it's important to have good manners in this rude world. But cultivating kindness means *taking practical and sacrificial actions to meet the needs of vulnerable people.*

According to the late professor, Rodney Stark, kindness was not a virtue in the culture where Christianity began:

> [In] the pagan world, and especially among the philosophers, mercy was regarded as a character defect and pity as a pathological emotion: because mercy involves providing unearned help or relief, it is contrary to justice. As E. A. Judge explained, classical philosophers taught that "mercy indeed is not governed by reason at all," and humans must learn "to

---

[*] Sources for this illustration: Rebecca Harrington, "I've donated my hair to charity 4 times, but I probably never will again. Here's what you need to know if you want to do it," *Business Insider*, Jan 28, 2023, https://businessinsider.com/donating-hair-to-charity-what-you-need-to-know-2016-12, accessed June 22, 2025. Mike Kilen, "The Kindest Cut of All," The Nashville *Tennessean*, October 17, 1998, found in *Proclaim!* Winter 1999-2000, page 30.

curb the impulse"; "the cry of the undeserving for mercy" must go "unanswered." Judge continued: "Pity was a defect of character unworthy of the wise and excusable only in those who have not yet grown up." [*]

But Paul taught that once we understand God's kindness to us in our need, we can't help but imitate that kindness to others in need.

We find a good example of this quality in a woman named Dorcas. In the Acts of the Apostles (9:32-42, NIV), we're told she was "always doing good and helping the poor." When she died, the disciples informed Simon Peter, the leader of the early church. He entered the room where her body had been prepared for burial, and all the widows "stood around him, crying and showing him the robes and other clothing that Dorcas had made while she was still with them." Peter "got down on his knees and prayed." After speaking to God, he spoke to the body and told Dorcas to get up. She did, and this "became known all over Joppa, and many people believed in the Lord."

This remarkable story can help us understand the virtue of kindness: Who needs our kindness, what results from our kindness, and how do we cultivate it?

## WHO NEEDS OUR KINDNESS?

It's the vulnerable who need our kindness. Dorcas "was always doing good and helping the poor" (Acts 9:36, NIV).

---

[*] Rodney Stark, *The Triumph of Christianity: How the Jesus Movement Became the World's Largest Religion* (New York : HarperOne, 2011), 112, quoting E.A. Judge, "The Quest for Mercy in Late Aniquity," in *God Who Is Rich in Mercy: Essays Presented to D.B. Knox*, edited by P.T. O'Brien and D.G. Peterson, (Sydney: Macquarie Univ. Press, 1986, 107-21.

As I said, when we see the word "kindness" as a fruit of the Spirit, we assume Paul was telling us not to be offensive. Growing up, when our parents told us to "be kind," they meant, "Don't fight with your sister. Don't be rude and ugly on the playground."

God doesn't want us to be rude or offensive to each other. But when Paul said, "The fruit of the Spirit is kindness," he was talking about something else.

In Proverbs 19:17 (NIV), we read, "Whoever is kind to the poor lends to the Lord, and he will reward them for what they have done."

When you help vulnerable people in practical and sacrificial ways, you're kind.

There's a soup kitchen in your city that could use your help. There's an elementary school that could use you as a reading mentor for children who are behind in their reading skills. There's a food drive that needs your donations. There's a disaster relief ministry that could use your skills as they help people rebuild after a storm. There's a pregnancy care center where you can provide the things that make it easier for women who decide to keep their babies—diapers, baby clothes, and other practical items.

All of this is what the Bible calls "kindness."

This doesn't mean we must respond to every panhandler. That's not possible, and it's often not helpful. But Dorcas demonstrated the impulse that should beat in every believer's heart: we must respond to the needs of vulnerable people in practical and sacrificial ways.

## WHAT RESULTS FROM OUR KINDNESS?

Sacrificial generosity gets noticed. It's not our motivation—we'll look at the motivation for kindness in a moment. But the biblical writers repeatedly pointed out how meeting the needs of others makes an impression.

Let's notice who notices.

*First, those who benefit from our kindness will take note.*

I read about a woman who called a florist to order flowers for a neighbor's funeral. The florist asked what message she wanted on the card. The woman had not thought about a message, and she said, "Well, I guess, 'You will be missed.'"

When she visited the funeral home the next day, she was mortified to see that the card accompanying her flowers had her exact words: "I guess you will be missed."*

Dorcas was missed, no question about it. When Simon Peter walked into the room where they had prepared her body, all these widows whom she had helped were gathered, showing Peter the garments the woman had made for them.

Widows were particularly vulnerable in that day and age. There were no pension plans or Social Security programs. When a breadwinner died, the wife often became destitute and exploited. Dorcas made sure the widows in her orbit were taken care of.

There's something intimate and personal about making clothing. Clothing for a tall person won't fit a short person. Clothing for a trim person won't fit a plus-size person. Dorcas likely had to do some measurements of each widow she worked with and then adjust the garments after the woman tried them on.

There was no greater eulogy that anyone could give than the one provided by these widows who showed Simon Peter what she had done for them.

I'm not implying that we should show kindness so that people will say nice things about us after we're gone. What

---

* From *Reader's Digest*, June 1994.

I'm saying is that people can't help but notice this characteristic.

*Second, when we're kind, the nonbelieving world pays attention.*

Simon Peter, the one who prayed for Dorcas to be restored to life, later wrote, "Friends, live such good lives among the nations that, though they accuse you of wrongdoing, they will see your *good deeds* and glorify God on the day he visits us" (1 Peter 2:11-12, NIV. Emphasis added).

As we go about obeying God in showing kindness to those in need, the world might say, "That impresses me. I may not like their rules on sexuality, but I've got to admit they're the first on the scene and the last to leave after a disaster. I may not like what they teach about gender differences, but I've got to admit they're on the front lines of ending sex trafficking. I can't deny that our community food banks and homeless shelters would have to shut down without their donations and volunteers."

In his book, *The Rise of Christianity,* Rodney Stark sought to explain how Christianity jumped from less than 8 percent of the Roman Empire to nearly 50 percent in just a century. He attributed much of the shift to how Christians responded to two major plagues. While even physicians and pagan priests fled the cities to avoid the contagion, Christians stayed and ministered—to Christians and pagans alike.*

Later, when the emperor, Julian, tried to revive the Roman pagan religion that was giving way to the rapid spread of Christianity, he unsuccessfully advised temple priests to adopt the Christian practice of charity. "Nothing has contributed to the progress of the superstition of the Christians as their

---

* Quoted in Colin Hansen, *Timothy Keller: His Spiritual and Intellectual Formation* (Grand Rapids: Zondervan, 2023), 225-26.

charity to strangers," he wrote. "The impious Galileans provide not only for their own poor, but for ours as well."\*

So, who notices our kindness? The people we help do, and so does the outside world.

*Third, God notices our kindness.*

In Acts 9, Peter's prayer that God would restore Dorcas to life came right after the widows' evidence of the woman's practical kindness. I'm not implying that the kinder you are to others in need, the more likely you are to be healed when someone prays. We all know generous people who left this world too soon and stingy misers who lived to old age.

But doesn't the Bible tell us that all of us will be raised to resurrection glory one day? Simon Peter called Dorcas by name and said, "Get up." Jesus will do the same for us. At the resurrection, he'll call us by name and say, "Get up."

That's when God will reward us for our earthly kindness, according to the Lord's own words:

> "When you give a luncheon or dinner, do not invite your friends, your brothers or sisters, your relatives, or your rich neighbors; if you do, they may invite you back and so you will be repaid. But when you give a banquet, invite the poor, the crippled, the lame, the blind, and you will be blessed. Although they cannot repay you, **you will be repaid at the resurrection of the righteous**" (Luke 14:12-14, NIV. Emphasis added).

The story of Dorcas is just a little foretaste of what's going to happen when Jesus raises *all* his people to eternal life and

---

\* Quoted in Timothy Keller, *Generous Justice: How God's Grace Makes Us Just* (New York: Dutton, 2010), 141.

then rewards us for the kindness we showed to vulnerable people.

## HOW DO WE CULTIVATE IT?

If kindness is so consequential, how do we cultivate it? The story of Dorcas helps us here, too.

The first thing we're told about her is not that she made garments for widows and helped the poor. The first thing we're told about her is that she was a *disciple*.

In his commentary on Acts, John Calvin wrote, "The title 'disciple' ... is the highest commendation, this is the beginning of a holy life, this is the root of all virtues, to have learned from the Son of God the way to live and what true life is. *The fruits of doing good follows....* So the description of [Dorcas] shows us reverence for God, or faith, coming first, and then ... meeting the needs of the poor."[*]

So, Dorcas didn't just show kindness; she was a *disciple* who showed kindness.

Like her, we show kindness the more we grasp that we are disciples to whom Christ has shown kindness. Paul wrote, "When the *kindness* and love of God our Savior appeared, he saved us, not because of righteous things we had done, but because of his mercy" (Titus 2:4-5, NIV).

He saw us as poor, vulnerable indigents under the consequences of our sin, and "though he was rich, yet for your sake he became poor, so that you through his poverty might become rich" (2 Corinthians 8:9, NIV).

He entered into our world, became one of us, and bore

---

[*] John Calvin, *Commentary Upon the Acts of the Apostles*, Christian Classics Ethereal Library, https://ccel.org/ccel/calvin/calcom36/calcom36.xvi.ix.html, accessed 24 June 2025. Emphasis added.

away our sin on the cross. Our care for others springs from that appreciation.

The cross isn't just the instrument by which God saved you; the cross is the instrument by which God reforms everything about your life. Whenever the New Testament tells us to do something, we're taken to the cross for our example and motivation.

So, for example, in Ephesians 5, Paul said, "Here's how to have a good marriage: Think about what Christ did for you and imitate that sacrificial love in your marriage." Again, in Ephesians 4:32 (NIV), he said to forgive others "just as in Christ God forgave you."

So, we shouldn't be surprised to see the cross used as a teaching tool for explaining why we should be compassionate to others. The Apostle John wrote, "Jesus Christ laid down his life for us. And we ought to lay down our lives for our brothers and sisters" (1 John 3:16, NIV). Then he explained what laying down our lives looks like: "If anyone has material possessions and sees a brother or sister in need but has no pity on them, how can the love of God be in that person?" (1 John 3:17, NIV.)

## "GET OUT!"

As Christianity began to spread beyond its Jewish origin into the surrounding culture, missionaries and pastors had to train new believers in a compassion that they were unaccustomed to.

John Stott pointed out that Roman Catholic communion is often called "the Mass" because of the final sentence in the old Latin rite: *ite missa est*. He wrote:

In polite English it might be rendered "Now you are dismissed." In more blunt language it could be just "Get out!" – out into the world which God made and God-like beings inhabit, the world into which Christ came and into which he now sends us. For that is where we belong. The world is the arena in which we are to live and love, witness and serve, suffer and die for Christ.*

We must show the kindness Christ has shown to us. *Ite missa est.* Now you are dismissed.

*"JESUS, YOU'VE BEEN SO KIND TO ME IN MY SPIRITUAL NEED. Help me to imitate that kindness in the way I relate to others in physical need. Amen."*

---

* John Stott, *Decisive Issues Facing Christians Today* (Old Tappan, N.J.: F.H. Revell, 1990), 26.

## CHAPTER 6

# MEET CUTE

*"The fruit of the Spirit is goodness"*

The true, the good, and the beautiful. Philosophers call them the *transcendentals,* and they've argued for millennia about how to define and develop them.

We need models as much as definitions, though, and that introduces a problem. Where can we find compelling exhibits of the transcendentals?

Creators will tell you that it's easier to portray evil characters than profoundly good characters. Writers like J.K. Rowling, Aaron Sorkin, Stephen King, and George R.R. Martin have discussed the challenge of writing noble characters as opposed to evil ones.

C. S. Lewis explained why:

> To make a character worse than oneself it is only necessary to release imaginatively from control some of the bad passions which, in real life, are always straining at the leash.... But ... we do not really know what it feels like to be a man

much better than ourselves.... To project ourselves into a good [character] we have to do what we cannot and become what we are not.*

The story of Ruth and Boaz is exceptional. It's a compelling story about two good people and how they found each other.

Here's how the Bible introduces us to Boaz: "Now Naomi had a relative on her husband's side. He was a prominent man *of noble character* from Elimelech's family" (Ruth 2:1, CSB).

Later in the story, Boaz described Ruth in the same way: "Now don't be afraid, my daughter. I will do for you whatever you say, since all the people in my town know that you are a woman *of noble character*" (Ruth 3:11, CSB).

The Hebrew word we translate as "noble character" has a range of meanings, but for Ruth and Boaz, it was a word about their goodness.

## THREE MARKS OF GOODNESS

What does it mean to be known for your goodness? Three things.

- *Integrity*: doing what is right to do; living by a moral code.

- *Restraint*: not exploiting others or taking advantage of a situation for your own gain.

---

* C.S. Lewis, "A Preface to Paradise Lost," in *Milton: Modern Essays in Criticism*, edited by Arthur E. Barker, Oxford University Press, 1965, pp. 92-100.

- *Altruism*: doing things that advantage others even if they disadvantage you.

In the story of Ruth and Boaz, from first to last, you see two people of integrity, restraint, and altruism.

What makes this more remarkable is the setting. The story of Ruth happened during a dark period of Israel's early history when "there was no king in Israel" and "everyone did whatever seemed right to him" (Judges 21:25 CSB). It was a time of moral relativism, decay, and anarchy.

It's hard enough to find a person of noble character in the best of times, but these were the worst of times. For two people like Ruth and Boaz to even *exist* in such a culture was rare; for these two good people to *find each other* in such a culture was astonishing.

Ruth was a Moabite. She entered the history of Israel when an Israelite named Naomi, along with her husband and two sons, moved to Moab to escape a famine. Ruth married one of Naomi's sons.

Then tragedy struck. Ruth's husband, father-in-law, and brother-in-law each died in separate incidents, leaving Naomi and her two daughters-in-law destitute.

Naomi decided to return to her home in Bethlehem, and Ruth chose to accompany her. It was an act of loyalty because it meant leaving her own home and culture. It's the first indication of Ruth's noble character.

They arrived in Bethlehem at the harvest season, and Ruth joined the indigents who survived by following the harvesters to glean the leftovers.

I love how the seventeenth-century King James Version puts it here: "her hap was to light on a part of the field belonging unto Boaz" (Ruth 2:3, KJV). *Her hap was to light.* In other words, she just happened to show up in a part of the field belonging to a family member of Naomi's late husband. I'll explain why this was significant in a moment.

Although Ruth didn't know anything about Boaz, Boaz already knew a little about her, and he began to show her special favor. He invited her to move up from the gleaners to join the harvesters themselves. This meant she would have better working conditions and could bring home more food for herself and Naomi.

His kindness to her was in response to her kindness to Naomi, who was part of his clan by marriage. Boaz appreciated this woman who showed such loyalty to a member of his family.

## CURIOUS COURTSHIP

Courtship shortly followed, and first-time readers find it unusual.

Of course, when it comes to ways that men and women show their interest in each other, cultural practices vary widely. Among the Welsh as far back as the 17th century, a young man would spend hours carving a "lovespoon" in hopes a girl would accept it from him. Finnish girls of marriageable age once wore an empty sheath on their girdle, and if a man presented a knife to put in her sheath, she could return it or keep it, depending on whether she was interested in him. Rural Austrians in the 1800s had a most unusual courtship practice. Eligible women would hold an apple slice in their armpits during dances. If she fancied a man, she would offer him the sweaty fruit and, if the feeling were mutual, he would eat it.*

Yum.

---

* Ethan Trex, "9 Strange Courtship Rituals From Around the World,"

Here's how the courtship of Ruth and Boaz began. While Boaz slept in the granary to guard his harvest, she put on perfume and her best outfit, snuck into the granary, and lay at his feet. He woke to find her there, and she said, "Take me under your wing."

We would interpret such actions as seduction in our culture, but not in that cultural context. When Ruth first arrived in Bethlehem, she was still mourning as a widow. So, Boaz, this man of noble character, had kept his distance from Ruth because he respected her condition. How would Ruth signal to him that her time of mourning was over and she was available to marry? In that culture, she did it by freshening herself and putting on perfume. That's also why she lay down beside him the way she did. It was the place a wife would lie in that culture if they were married.

Although it wasn't an act of sexual seduction, that doesn't mean her plan had no risk. If she had misjudged his character, Boaz could have taken advantage of her. But she determined that this man could be trusted, and so she took steps that he would have interpreted as a request that he marry her.

Boaz was all too happy to marry her. There was just one snag. Another man in Boaz's family had the responsibility to take this widowed woman in marriage.

In that culture, when a woman lost her husband, someone from her dead husband's family was responsible for marrying her. This served two purposes: the widow and any orphans would be cared for, and the property of the dead man would be preserved for his family line.

This was the role of the "family redeemer." He did all the work of managing the dead husband's field and raising the

*Mental Floss*, November 4, 2015, https://www.mentalfloss.com/article/28950/9-strange-courtship-rituals-around-world. Accessed 26 June 2025.

dead husband's children, but he wouldn't get any financial reward from it.

The man who was first in line to be the family redeemer was unwilling to bear this cost, and so he refused to marry Ruth. But Boaz did what was right and played the role of family redeemer no matter what it would cost him. Ruth and Boaz got married, had a son, and their part in the story ended happily.

It's not the end of the story, as we'll see in a minute, but it's the end of their part in the story.

Before we get to the ultimate end of the story, let's go back to the three identifying marks of goodness. A person filled with goodness has integrity, restraint, and altruism.

Ruth and Boaz displayed *integrity*. They stuck to their obligations and didn't quit. They had a strong work ethic and were industrious, not only for their own sake but because they had people depending on them.

Ruth and Boaz each showed *restraint*, too. Restraint means you're not taking advantage of others for your own ends. Boaz didn't take advantage of Ruth, and he took measures to make sure that other men wouldn't assault her, either. For Ruth's part, though she could have had the pick of any man, her decision to ask Boaz to marry her though he was much older was an act of restraint against emotional recklessness. (See Ruth 3:10.)

Finally, Ruth and Boaz each displayed *altruism*. The word means doing things for the good of others, even if it disadvantages you.

Their altruism shows up in sharp contrast to others in the story. The book of Ruth *begins* with two daughters-in-law and *ends* with two family redeemers. Because of this, we get a chance to see the character of Ruth and Boaz played out against people with lesser character.

- At the beginning of the story, two young women married into Naomi's family, but only Ruth stayed loyal to her dead husband's mother when everything came apart.

- At the end of the story, there were two family redeemers, but only Boaz was willing to fulfill his obligation at great cost to himself.

Boaz and Ruth were each marked by integrity, restraint, and altruism, and they admired these qualities in each other.

Now, the point of their story isn't that if you just work on a life of goodness, eventually you'll find someone to marry who is just as committed to a life of goodness. One thing we learn from the story of Boaz and Ruth is just how rare it is for two good people to find each other in this dark world. But God brought them together against all odds.

## MUCH MORE THAN A LOVE STORY

God brought them together for a purpose much larger than just their own happiness. It certainly makes God happy to see his people happy, but the story of Boaz and Ruth doesn't end with the line, "And they lived happily ever after."

How does it end? With a genealogy. A genealogy that leads straight to King David, the most beloved king of Israel.

The book begins with God's people in the days without a king—a time of anarchy, immorality, and idolatry. Four chapters later, the book ends with the name of Israel's greatest king: "David."

What does that tell us? No matter how dark things look now, God is always working to fix what we mess up.

But there's more. A thousand years after Ruth and Boaz

and their grandson David, a Christian disciple named Matthew took this same genealogy that ended the book of Ruth, and he extended it. He continued the family line past Israel's greatest king to the birth of the King of Kings.

The first six verses that open the Gospel of Matthew copy the last five verses of the Book of Ruth almost word for word. But then Matthew continued the genealogy from David up to the birth of Jesus in Bethlehem, the same town where Ruth and Boaz fell in love.

The love story of Ruth and Boaz is just preparation for us to appreciate the ultimate love story between Jesus and his bride, the church (Ephesians 5:25-32; Revelation 21:9-10).

We've looked at Ruth and Boaz as examples of goodness, but Jesus is the ultimate model of goodness—and that tells us something about his true identity.

Once a certain ruler asked Jesus, "Good teacher, what must I do to inherit eternal life?" Jesus replied, "Why do you call me good? No one is good—except God alone'" (Luke 18:18-19, NIV).

Was Jesus objecting to this characterization? Was he saying he wasn't good? Of course not.

Jesus invited this man to think through the implications of what he was saying. If this man saw unadulterated goodness in Jesus, and if God was the only being in the universe who could be good to that degree, what did that imply about Jesus?

It's subtle, but it's there: In Jesus, God came to visit us. In Jesus, God entered our world.

*The very Jesus born from the line of Ruth and Boaz was the God who had supernaturally enabled Ruth and Boaz to find each other in the first place.*

And yet God entered this world for a purpose. This good man Jesus willingly died for people who are not good so that we might be saved. Jesus is the true and better Boaz. Jesus is our family redeemer who paid the price of his own life to set us free from sin.

The Apostle Paul wrote, "Christ died for the ungodly. For rarely will someone die for a just person—though for a *good* person perhaps someone might even dare to die. But God proves his own love for us in that *while we were still sinners*, Christ died for us" (Romans 5:6-8, NIV. Emphasis added).

## HOW SHOULD WE THEN LIVE?

It's inspiring to read about the goodness of Ruth and Boaz, but it's convicting, too. Remember our definition of goodness: integrity, restraint, and altruism. Do those words characterize you? Always? If not, what should you do?

First, repent. Admit to our good God that you have failed at goodness. You don't have to stay mired in regret; you don't have to wallow in shame. "If we confess our sins, he is faithful and just and will forgive us our sins and purify us from all unrighteousness" (1 John 1:9). So, repent. Trust that the death of Jesus was sufficient to free you from condemnation.

And then, second, aspire. Aspire to the goodness you haven't reached yet. Paul called it fruit: "The fruit of the Spirit is goodness." The word "fruit" implies a process: fruit is the end result of a process. Just because you haven't shown much integrity, restraint, or altruism in the past doesn't mean people won't think of you in those terms in the future. Aspire to get there, ask the Spirit of Jesus to do his good work in your life every day, and people will start seeing goodness in you like they saw in Ruth and Boaz.

Authors and screenwriters often find it harder to write about good people than evil people. But in real life, we prefer them. Let's aspire to be the kind of people we want to have around.

.   .   .

*JESUS, YOU ONCE INVITED A MAN TO EXPLAIN WHY HE CALLED you good. We know. As we learned in our first childhood prayer, God is great, and God is good—and your perfect goodness reveals who you are. You are the very embodiment of the God who is good. After all our many failures to act with goodness, we repent of our failures in confidence that your sacrifice makes us clean, and we aspire to become who you want us to be: good. Amen."*

## CHAPTER 7

# THE POWER OF PLODDING

*"The fruit of the Spirit is faithfulness"*

The kingdom of God doesn't advance just through important people doing important things in important places. It advances through the work of average people doing the average but necessary things week in and week out.

People like Malchijah.

Who?

Exactly.

I bet you've never heard a sermon about Malchijah. I bet you've never read a book that featured him. His one-sentence claim to fame is found in the middle of an Old Testament chapter you don't remember reading.

When the Israelites returned from the Babylonian exile, they needed to rebuild the wall around Jerusalem. *Everything* needed rebuilding, of course, because Babylon had destroyed it all. But Nehemiah knew that the walls had to come first.

The nation's pride and protection depended on it. So, Nehemiah rallied the people to rebuild the walls.

Lots of leadership books and seminars focus on the leadership principles from Nehemiah. But he never would have succeeded without the ordinary people listed in chapter three.

For thirty-two verses, we have this long list of those who joined Nehemiah in the work. It's simply a list of names and what portion of the wall they built.

The list begins and ends at the same place: the Sheep Gate. It's as if the writer were taking us on a guided tour around the perimeter of Jerusalem, pointing out the contributors along the way: "So-and-so built this section from here to here, and then so-and-so built this section from here to here." And at the end of the chapter, we're back where we started. Jerusalem had been fully enclosed with a protective wall.

## THE DUNG GATE GUY

Many of the sections of the wall were described by the gates they adjoined. So, you have one man celebrated for rebuilding the section at the Sheep Gate, another man honored for rebuilding the section at the Fish Gate, another one remembered for rebuilding the section near the Valley Gate, and so on.

Then we get to Malchijah's contribution: "Malchijah son of Rechab, ruler of the district of Beth-haccherem, repaired the Dung Gate. He rebuilt it and installed its doors, bolts, and bars" (Nehemiah 3:14, CSB).

He wasn't the only Malchijah in the list. The name must have been a common name back then. But here's a big difference between the two men with the same name. The Malchijah in verse 11 had the task of building the wall near the

Tower of the Ovens, while the Malchijah in verse 14 had the task of building the wall near the Dung Gate.

The Tower of the Ovens was a reference to a bakery. Have you ever lived near a bakery?

A man in our church once told me that when he and his wife were newlyweds, she worked at a pastry shop. One day after she came home from a morning shift, he gave her a long, lingering hug.

"Someone's glad to see me," she said.

He sighed contentedly. "You smell like donuts."

The Malchijah of verse 11 got that pleasant smell every day near the place where he repaired the wall.

But the Malchijah of verse 14? He worked with a different aroma wafting by. His assignment was to build the wall beside the Dung Gate.

Now, that passageway was an important part of the sacrificial system. When animals were sacrificed at the Temple, the entrails and other unclean parts of the animal had to be removed in such a way that the material wouldn't defile the place. And so, the Dung Gate was a necessary part of God's design for the Temple.

Still, if you were to get just one mention in the Bible, would you want to be known as the Dung Gate Guy?

But what would have happened had no one stepped up to build that little part of the wall? Even if every other part of the wall got built, had that one spot been left alone, the whole city would have remained vulnerable. Nothing's as useless as an incomplete wall.

Malchijah should make us all ask ourselves, "Where is my bit of wall I'm responsible for? How can I do my little part for God's kingdom?"

Faithfulness is a superpower. If you just do what needs to

be done, they'll never make a Marvel movie about your life, but you have a superpower.

## RADICAL INDIVIDUALISM

Now, if faithfulness is a superpower, two things act like kryptonite against this superpower. The first is *radical individualism*.

The theme song for some Christians would have to be Tom T. Hall's, *Me and Jesus*:

> *Well, me and Jesus got our own thing goin'*
> *Me and Jesus got it all worked out*
> *Me and Jesus got our own thing goin'*
> *We don't need anybody to tell us what it's all about**

Oh, you may regard it as a useful option to connect with other Christians in a church. But it's all based on what a church can do for you, not what you can do with and for a congregation. That's part of what's behind the increase in Christians reporting no affiliation with a particular church.

But it's hard to convince Jesus that we love him if we don't care about what's important to him. And "Christ loved the church and gave himself up for her" (Ephesians 5:25, NIV). Jesus is crazy in love with his church. Those who love him will love what he loves.

Malchijah strikes a blow against our radical individualism. Nehemiah 3 is one of the most corporate chapters in the whole Bible. What I mean is, it's not about individuals just doing their own thing, but individuals all contributing to the

---

* Tom T. Hall, "Me and Jesus," from the 1972 album, *We All Get Together And...*.

common good. *It's about men and women who signed on to a project much larger than themselves for the sake of a people important to God.*

That's a perfect picture of the way the New Testament writers wanted us to love the church. God did not call us to radical individualism--just "me and Jesus."

## GRANDIOSITY

We can't be faithful to the work of God's kingdom if we're infected with radical individualism. But some of us are fine with being in a group project—at least if it's grand and earth-shaking.

We're desperate to be extraordinary. Lore Ferguson Wilbert wrote:

> I am of the "Don't waste your life!" generation, a generation of young people in the church who believed their greatest call was to not settle for mediocrity in their Christian life.... Passion was the proof of salvation, zeal was the evidence of our faith, "Send me!" was our mantra, and "world changers" was our identity. *We all wanted to be used by God, but none of us wanted to fold up the chairs afterward.* *

That's a good observation.

Malchijah didn't suffer from grandiosity. It would have been easy for him to do so, because he was an important person in the community. I don't know if you noticed it on your first reading of the verse, but Malchijah was "ruler of the

---

* Lore Ferguson Wilbert, "Those God Sends, He First Humbles" *Christianity Today*, September 2022, https://www.christianitytoday.com/2022/08/curious-faith-questions-lore-ferguson-wilbert/, accessed 7 July 2025. Emphasis added.

district of Beth Hakkerem" (Nehemiah 3:14, CSB). A ruler forever identified as the Dung Gate Guy! Many who reach a certain level of importance in the world would be reluctant to take on a job like that.

## THE POWER OF PLODDING

Radical individualism and grandiosity. Those things are common today, but Malchijah had neither of those problems. He was a perfect example of the power of plodding.

Kevin DeYoung wrote:

> What we need are fewer revolutionaries and a few more plodding visionaries. That's my dream for the church—a multitude of faithful, risktaking plodders. The best churches are full of gospel-saturated people holding tenaciously to a vision of godly obedience and God's glory, and pursuing that godliness and glory with relentless, often unnoticed, plodding consistency.... Until we are content with being one of the million nameless, faceless church members and not the next globe-trotting rock star, we aren't ready to be a part of the church.... In all the smallness and sameness, God works —like the smallest seed in the garden growing to unbelievable heights, like beloved Tychicus, that faithful minister, delivering the mail and apostolic greetings (Eph. 6:21). Life is usually pretty ordinary, just like following Jesus most days. Daily discipleship is not a new revolution each morning or an agent of global transformation every evening; it's a long obedience in the same direction.*

---

* Kevin DeYoung, "The Glory of Plodding," *TableTalk*, Ligonier Ministries, May 1, 2010, https://learn.ligonier.org/articles/glory-plodding, accessed 7 July 2025.

When DeYoung wrote about "plodding visionaries," I don't know if he had William Carey in mind. But it's easy to think he did.

William Carey was born in a small, rural village in England in the eighteenth century. He apprenticed in a local cobbler's shop, and when he was converted, he borrowed a Greek grammar book and taught himself New Testament Greek. He proved proficient at languages, and soon he added Hebrew and Latin to his self-taught studies. He also continued pursuing his lifelong interest in international affairs and developed a burden for missions.

Carey became a Baptist pastor, and in 1792, he organized a missionary society. Soon, the pastor who talked to others about missions surrendered to his own challenge, and he took his wife and children to India.

Carey's early years there were miserable. The one other man who had come with him deserted the enterprise, illness racked the family, and loneliness and regret set in. At one point, William Carey wrote in his diary: "I am in a strange land. No Christian friend, a large family, and nothing to supply their wants." But then he added: "Well, I have God, and his word is sure."

When Carey himself contracted malaria, and then his five-year-old Peter died of dysentery, it became too much for his wife, Dorothy. Her mental health deteriorated rapidly. She suffered paranoid delusions, threatening her husband with a knife on one occasion. She eventually had to be confined to a room and physically restrained.

In his diary, Carey wrote, "This is indeed the valley of the shadow of death to me. But I rejoice that I am here notwithstanding; and God is here."

He learned Bengali with the help of a local, and in a few weeks began translating the Bible into Bengali and preaching to small gatherings. In December 1800, after seven years of missionary labor, Carey baptized his first convert. Two months later, he published his first Bengali New Testament.

But hardships as well as progress continued. One of the most devastating setbacks was a warehouse fire in 1812. By then, he had created a massive dictionary, two grammar books, and whole versions of the Bible in various Indian languages. All of it was destroyed, and no backup copies existed. Carey accepted the tragedy as from the Lord and began all over again with even greater zeal.

He never took a furlough back home to England. He stayed in India for 40 years, translating the entire Bible into India's six major languages, and parts of the Bible into 209 other languages and dialects.

How was he able to do it? He once wrote: "I can plod. I can persevere to any definite pursuit. To this I owe everything."

Carey was an eighteenth-century Malchijah. Now it's your turn to be a twenty-first-century Malchijah.

Who knows? You may be remembered like the famous Nehemiah. But that's not the destiny of most of us. Most of us will be called to stand shoulder to shoulder with others and just build our little bit of wall for the glory of God's cause.

So, young mom: keep bringing your kids to church. You're building your little bit of the wall.

Children's worker: keep pouring God's word into those lives. You're building your little bit of the wall.

Nursery volunteer: keep changing those diapers and doing what it takes to make those young parents confident to put their child in your care. You're building your little bit of the wall.

Faithful giver: Keep contributing. Faithful pray-er: Keep

praying. Faithful small-group leader: Keep contacting the prospects and absentees. You're building your little bit of the wall.

## WASHING FEET

Malchijah did what was necessary in service to the people of God. Jesus demonstrated this supremely in his sacrifice.

In the Gospel of John, we read that the night before Jesus went to the cross, at the Lord's Supper he knelt down and washed the feet of his men. In those days, footwashing was part of hospitality. People walked everywhere and they had open sandals, so before they stepped too far into a house, they needed the dust and mud off their feet. Washing feet was the job given to the lowliest servant, and yet when Jesus saw how none of this apostles wanted to do this for each other, he took a washbasin and towel and did the work himself.

He did this for two reasons that become clear as you read the story. First, he was preparing them to understand the meaning of the cross. Just as he washed their feet that night, the next day he would cleanse their souls of sin by the work of the cross. But then he said to them, "Now that I, your Lord and Master have washed your feet, you wash each other's feet." In other words, we're to serve each other like Jesus served us.

Maybe you need to let Jesus serve you by saving you. Once we're served by him in this way, it will be easier to serve others—even if it means being forever known as the Dung Gate Guy.

*"JESUS, I PRAY FOR THOSE WHO NEED TO ACCEPT YOUR SERVICE for them. The message of Christianity isn't about what we must do to*

*prove our love to you, but what you did out of your love for us. I also pray for those who have received your service for us and now we need to serve others like you did. Like Malchijah, help us be willing to do whatever needs doing, and do it well, in a long obedience in the same direction. Amen."*

# CHAPTER 8

## GETTING YOURSELF OFF
## YOUR HANDS

*"The fruit of the Spirit is humility"*

You might remember Jim Collins' bestselling book, *Good to Great*. It was the product of intense research into how certain underperforming companies became incredibly profitable.

The research found that every company that went from good to great had a certain kind of leader. Collins called them "Level 5" leaders. I won't go into his description of the lower levels, but here's how he defined a Level 5 leader:

They display a powerful mixture of personal humility and indomitable will. They're incredibly ambitious, but their ambition is first and foremost for the cause, for the organization and its purpose, not themselves. While Level 5 leaders can come in many personality packages, they are often self-effacing, quiet, reserved, and even shy. *

He said that this was a counterintuitive finding because "people generally assume that transforming companies from good to great requires larger-than-life leaders—big personalities ... who make headlines and become celebrities." Not so. While lesser leaders are busy making a name for themselves and getting on the cover of business journals for their big, dominant personalities, Level 5 leaders are the ones who build companies that last.

In his list of the fruit of the Spirit, the Apostle Paul had a word for this character trait.

His Greek word, *prautes*, is translated into English using the words *meekness*, *gentleness*, or *humility*.

In these chapters, we're examining characters from the Bible who demonstrated Paul's nine noble virtues. The life of Moses can help us understand the characteristic of humility.

In Numbers 12:3 (NIV), we read, "Moses was a very humble man, more humble than anyone else on earth."

It might surprise you to read that Moses had this quality. If you know even a little about his biography, you might describe him with words like *leader*, *stern*, *strong*, or *focused*. You would likely compile a long list of other words before it occurred to you to call him gentle and humble.

But maybe that's because we've misunderstood this characteristic.

---

* "Level 5 Leadership," https://www.jimcollins.com/concepts/level-five-leadership.html, accessed 7 July 2025.

## WHAT IS HUMILITY?

Behaviors that we regard as examples of humility may be nothing of the sort.

We tend to label someone as humble if they're unintimidating, or if they're soft-spoken, or if they always give way to the preferences of others.

But if you looked *under* the behaviors, you may not find humility driving the actions. Some people are unintimidating because they lack courage. Some people can be soft-spoken to avoid confrontation. Growing up in a dysfunctional family, they learned how messy it can be, so they avoid it. Some people can let everyone have their way because they want to be seen as the martyr in the relationship. They let everyone have their way, but inside they seethe with resentment.

So, just having the behaviors doesn't mean you have the inner characteristic Paul called humility.

The quality Paul had in mind is the state where you're finally free from yourself. Your ego no longer runs the show. You're no longer patrolling the ramparts, protecting your self-worth from every little threat. You don't get defensive and prickly every time someone has a complaint against you.

Moses showed this quality of true gentleness in the face of bitter attacks: "Moses had married a Cushite woman, and Miriam and Aaron criticized him for it. They said, 'Has the Lord spoken only through Moses? Hasn't he also spoken through us?'" (Numbers 12:1-2, NIV.)

They struck at three things. First, they belittled his family. They began to talk against Moses because of his wife. Scholars are divided: some say that this refers to a new wife he married after he became a widower. I tend to agree with other scholars who say the wife in question is Zipporah, to whom Moses had been married for forty years. If that's the case, their disapproval of her had simmered under the surface in the family dynamics for decades. Sometimes that happens in families.

Either way, they complained against her because she was a Cushite. That means she came from an area on the map we now call Ethiopia. So, Miriam and Aaron complained about this woman who was so racially and culturally different from them.

Second, they belittled his competence. Since he had married someone whom they disapproved of, they concluded that there must be something wrong with his judgment.

And third, they questioned his authority. Now we get to the heart of the matter. In their mind, his marriage to this woman was a sign that Moses needed to be managed. He needed second-guessing, and they were the ones to do it.

What must have made this all the more painful for Moses was that Miriam and Aaron were family and ministry partners. They were his older brother and sister who partnered with him to lead Israel out of Egyptian slavery toward the Promised Land. (See Micah 6:4.)

So, these weren't strangers or insignificant upstarts. These were family members and long-time partners in leadership.

It's hard enough when strangers attack your family, your competence, and your authority. It's devastating when those attacks come from those you thought had your back.

Everything about the first two verses in the story would make you think the next verse, verse 3, would go like this: "In response, Moses threw down on them. Moses popped off with a good insult and they got owned."

And yet we read, "Moses was very humble." He didn't react with rudeness, and he didn't get defensive. Even after the Lord cursed Miriam with a defiling skin disease (Numbers

12:12), Moses didn't say, "Serves you right." No, but he prayed for God to heal her.*

When someone reacts to criticism with rudeness or intimidation, what do we tend to think? "Now there's a man who knows how to defend himself. There's a woman who isn't going to let anyone walk all over her."

But even though their actions seem so strong and assertive, look behind their actions. You'll likely find insecurity, self-doubt, and fragile self-worth.

Moses had himself off his hands.

## WHY DO WE NEED TO DEVELOP HUMILITY?

Without this quality, you won't be able to preserve your *relationships* or complete your *responsibilities*.

**Your relationships**. One of the most common things that marriage counselors face in their clients is defensiveness. By the time a couple finally comes to the counselor, one or both parties have developed such a wall of defensiveness that it's very hard to get them to admit there's anything they need to change.

Therapists call this a maladaptive response technique. The behavior is "adaptive" in that we develop it over time as a response to constant criticism and belittling. But it's *mal*adaptive because it doesn't help us. It protects us in the short term, but it doesn't help the relationship thrive.

You're going to deal with complaints and criticism in your family, at work, and in church. Some of it will be fair, and a lot of it will be patently unfair. If you spend all your time and

---

* Don't misunderstand why she was punished with the medical condition and Aaron was spared. It wasn't because she was a woman who dared to question a male in authority. Instead, it was because, of the two, she was the instigator. Aaron participated in the rebellion, but Miriam led it.

energy getting defensive at every slight, you're going to end up a very lonely person.

**Your responsibilities**. Moses led a vast crowd of Israelites out of Egyptian slavery toward the Promised Land. But this challenge from Miriam and Aaron in Numbers 12 was just one of a long list of episodes where the Israelites second-guessed Moses, complained against him, and proved fickle in their opinion of him. Moses would not have accomplished all he did if he had spent all his time and energy trading insults for insults.

You may not be tasked with the job of leading a nation out of slavery, but there are things you're supposed to accomplish in your brief time on this earth. Just like Moses, you're not going to get very far with your responsibilities without this quality of gentleness and humility.

This is why we read this requirement of pastors: "The Lord's servant must not be quarrelsome but must be kind to everyone, able to teach, not resentful. Opponents must be *gently* instructed, in the hope that God will grant them repentance leading them to a knowledge of the truth, and that they will come to their senses and escape from the trap of the devil, who has taken them captive to do his will" (2 Timothy 2:24-26, NIV).

This Moses-like ability to get yourself off your hands isn't just for pastors, though. Paul reminded *all* of us, "Brothers and sisters, if someone is caught in a sin, you who live by the Spirit should restore that person *gently*" (Galatians 6:1, NIV). And Peter said this quality is required as we talk with the world about our faith: "Always be prepared to give an answer to everyone who asks you to give the reason for the hope that you have. But do this with *gentleness* and respect" (1 Peter 3:15, NIV).

None of the things God expects of you can get done if you

don't have this quality of humility and gentleness at the center of your being.

## HOW DO WE DEVELOP HUMILITY?

Whenever Jim Collins presents his findings on Level 5 leadership, someone always asks him how they can become this kind of leader. Among a range of things that might develop someone into a Level 5 Leader, he added this:

> A strong religious belief or conversion might also nurture the seed. Colman Mockler, for example [CEO of Gillette when the company transformed from good to great], converted to evangelical Christianity while getting his MBA at Harvard, and later, according to the book *Cutting Edge*, he became a prime mover in a group of Boston business executives that met frequently over breakfast to discuss the carryover of religious values to corporate life. *

Collins is not particularly religious, and he would not say that religious belief is the only thing that can make someone a Level 5 Leader. Still, there is something about living in the biblical story that can get you there.

The story the world says you're in goes like this: "Do the right things to be accepted." The story the Bible says you're in goes like this: "You're accepted, so do the right things."

As Moses heard the complaints about his capabilities from Miriam and Aaron, he probably agreed with them. After all, when God called him to lead the Israelites out of Egypt, he argued back with God about all the reasons he wasn't the

---

* "Can You Grow into Level 5 Leadership?" https://www.jimcollins.com/article_topics/articles/can-you-grow-into-level-5.html, accessed 7 July 2025.

right person for the job (Exodus 3:11; 4:10; 4:13). So, Moses didn't need to defend himself to his opponents. God defended him. God said, "This one's mine; I chose him; he's doing my work" (see Numbers 12:4-8).

Moses operated out of a keen awareness that God loved him and chose him. God's love for him and choice of him came first, and out of that came the performance. This is a completely different story from the world's story.

If you live by the world's story, you'll always be building and defending your resume. You'll always have to justify yourself. Since the world says, "Impress us enough and we'll accept you," you'll never feel that your self-worth is completely safe.

But the biblical story says, "God accepts you. He just does. For his own sake, for his own glory, he picked you for his team. Now live like that's true."

If we lived out of this story, we'd be freed from our need to perform for love and acceptance. We'd be freed from having to defend our ego and prop up our self-worth.

The Apostle Paul put it this way in one of his letters: "Long before he laid down earth's foundations, he had us in mind, had settled on us as the focus of his love, to be made whole and holy by his love" (Ephesians 1:4, Msg).

When did he settle on you as the focus of his love? *Long before he laid down the earth's foundations.* That means he decided to love you before you were born, let alone before you started doing anything useful for him.

Paul went on to explain the lengths God was willing to go for those he had decided to love from the start:

Long, long ago he decided to adopt us into his family through Jesus Christ. (What pleasure he took in planning this!) He wanted us to enter into the celebration of his lavish gift-giving by the hand of his beloved Son. Because of the sacrifice of the Messiah, his blood poured out on the altar of the Cross, we're a free people—free of penalties and punishments chalked up by all our misdeeds. And not just barely free, either. Abundantly free! He thought of everything, provided for everything we could possibly need, letting us in on the plans he took such delight in making. He set it all out before us in Christ, a long-range plan in which everything would be brought together and summed up in him, everything in deepest heaven, everything on planet earth. (Ephesians 1:5-10, Msg.)

When we consistently live out of this story, we're free! We're free from our need to perform for love and acceptance. We're free from our need to defend our ego and prop up our self-worth. And we're free to respond with gentleness and humility when other people express their opinion of us, fair or unfair.

I invite you into this biblical story of God's love. You'll spend the rest of your life learning to live in alignment with God's love for you, but it has to start somewhere. Let it be today.

*"FATHER, WHENEVER I'VE RESPONDED UNGRACIOUSLY TO ungracious criticism, it's always because I've forgotten that your opinion of me is the only opinion that ultimately matters. The world tells me, that as long as I perform well and don't screw up, they'll accept me or at least tolerate me. But you tell me I'm yours. Whatever I need to change about myself, whatever I need to repent of, it never changes the fact that you have chosen me, Lord. I pray for those who are still living the world's story. Bring them into your wonderful story*

*today. Let them see that the cross of Christ was how you set things right with us so that we can belong to you. In Jesus' name I pray. Amen."*

# CHAPTER 9

# THE WORLD'S WEAKEST
# STRONG MAN

*"The fruit of the Spirit is self-control"*

As we've seen, Paul's fruit of the Spirit included a few characteristics that the ancient Greco-Roman philosophers would not have considered virtues. Kindness and humility, for example.

But every list of virtues in the Greco-Roman world included self-control. Epictetus said, "No man is free who is not master of himself."[*] The Stoics included temperance among their four core values, which early Christian theologians also taught as the four "cardinal" virtues.[†]

Fruit such as peace and patience are necessary when life is

---

[*] "Epictetus on Self-Control: 10 Essential Stoic Quotes for Mastery," *Stoic*. https://www.getstoic.com/quotes/stoic-quotes-epictetus-self-control, accessed 10 July 2025.

[†] The four virtues are Wisdom (or Prudence), Courage, Temperance, Justice. In the early centuries of the Christian movement, theologians added what they called the "theological" virtues of faith, hope, and love, and taught seven key virtues.

going poorly, but self-control is a virtue for all times—"all the more necessary when times are good."[*] It's when we face an abundance of resources and options that we need it most.

In every other chapter in this book, we've looked at biblical characters who displayed the virtues under consideration.

Not in this chapter. We now turn to a perfect example of someone who lacked self-control. His name was Samson, and his story is found in Judges 13-16.

Samson could have been a character right out of a superhero movie. He had long, uncut hair and a massive build. His story reads like panels in a graphic novel. In one fight scene, we see how he single-handedly killed dozens of enemy soldiers, and then in another he killed a thousand all by himself. Then there was the time he yanked up the city gates of one enemy town and carried the whole contraption away on his shoulders.

But until his last repentant prayer, his entire life was "impulsive, spoiled, demanding, arrogant, and lacking judgment."[†]

## "WEAK EYES, WEAK HEART, CAN LOSE"

In the hit television show, *Friday Night Lights*, the Dillon Panthers football team had a slogan they frequently chanted in unison: "Clear eyes, strong hearts, can't lose!"

Samson had strong muscles, but ultimately he was a loser because his eyes and heart were frail.

---

[*] Andre Comte-Sponville, *A Small Treatise on the Great Virtues: The Use of Philosophy in Everyday* Life (New York: Picador, 2002), 42.
[†] Fred Smith, "Why God Still Works Through Fools Like Samson," *Christianity Today*, March 2018, https://www.christianitytoday.com/2018/02/why-god-still-works-through-fools-like-samson/, accessed 8 July 2025.

I'm not talking about the physical organs. In the story, his eyes and heart were representative of his judgment and longings.

**First, the biblical writer used Samson's eyes as a metaphor for poor judgment**. In the days before the kings, "everyone did whatever was right in their own *eyes*" (Judges 17:6; 21:25, ESV). Sadly, Samson was no different than the people he led. Samson chose his first wife because, as he put it, "she is right in my *eyes*" (Judges 14:3, ESV). To drive the point home, the metaphor reappears in verse 7 ("she was right in Samson's *eyes*").

God had forbidden his people to marry outside the faith, and this woman was among the pagan enemies of Israel. But Samson didn't make decisions based on God's word. He did what seemed right to him.

He was a man of poor judgment. Whatever he saw went straight into the mind without any discernment or processing.

Martin Luther said, "Temptations, of course, cannot be avoided, but because we cannot prevent the birds from flying over our heads, there is no need that we should let them nest in our hair."* We can't control the thoughts and images from flitting around us, but we can prevent them from taking up a home in us.

In the New Testament, the Apostle John warned about this: "For everything in the world—the lust of the flesh, the lust of the *eyes*, and the pride of life—comes not from the Father but from the world" (1 John 2:16, NIV. Emphasis added). When we see the word "lust" in that verse, we might think that John is warning us only about sexual matters. His

---

* Martin Luther, *Explanation of the Lord's Prayer*, Sixth Petition, paragraph 161, in *Luther's Catechetical Writings*, pages 304-05, https://ia600204.us.archive.org/3/items/lutherscatechetiooluth/lutherscatechetiooluth_bw.pdf, accessed 8 July 2025.

warning certainly included sexual intemperance, but he had in mind *any* craving that we have a hard time controlling. Items we don't really need to buy. Food we don't really need to eat. That one drink too many that we don't really need to order.

So, the eyes serve as a metaphor for disordered judgment in Samson's story. When we don't order or structure our judgment in alignment with the word of God, we won't have self-control.

**Second, the biblical writer used Samson's heart as a metaphor for disordered longings.**

After his disastrous first marriage ended, he squandered twenty years just sleeping with whomever his eyes landed on (Judges 16:1). But then we get to the first woman in the story with a name. It was as if the others were too insignificant to his story to get named, but then we come to Delilah. Not only are we told her name, but we're told he *loved* her (Judges 16:4). It's the first time in his biography that he loved anyone.

If the word "eyes" is pivotal to the first half of his story, the word "heart" is pivotal to Delilah's part of the story.

Samson's enemies had promised Delilah a lot of money if she could find out the source of his strength. He toyed around with her several times at first, giving her false reports of where his strength came from. She complained, "How can you say, 'I love you,' when your *heart* is not with me?" (Judges 16:15, ESV.) Finally, "he told her all his *heart*" (Judges 16:17, ESV). He explained that, because of a peculiar vow he was under, if his hair were shorn, "my strength will leave me, and I shall become weak and be like any other man." Now Delilah "saw that he had told her *all his heart*," and so she called the lords of the Philistines, saying, 'Come up again, for he has told me *all his heart*'" (Judges 16:18, ESV).

The word "heart" appears four times in four verses. It's hard to miss the point.

In our day, we tend to think of the heart as the wellspring of our *feelings*. To the biblical writers, the heart was the wellspring of our *longings*. Longings are more consequential than mere feelings. What you long for is what you believe will make you happy and secure. It determines everything you do, every choice you make, and every high joy or deep depression you endure.

The wise man wrote, "Above all else, guard your heart, for everything you do flows from it" (Proverbs 4:23, NIV).

Samson did not guard his heart. Getting and keeping this inadvisable relationship became everything to him. His longings were out of order.

What happened to Samson after he revealed the source of his strength? Delilah arranged for someone to cut off his hair while he slept with his head in her lap in complete trust. When he awoke to find himself surrounded by his enemies, he prepared to overpower them as he had always done. That's when the storyteller informs us that "he did not know that the Lord had left him" (Judges 16:20).

It's not that there was anything magical in his hair. His uncut hair was a symbol of a peculiar Nazirite vow. Those under such a vow were supposed to be in a special commitment to the Lord. But Samson had left God out of much of his life, and so God finally left him.

When his enemies saw that he had become powerless, they "seized him and gouged out his eyes and brought him down to Gaza and bound him with bronze shackles. And he ground at the mill in the prison" (Judges 16:21).

The mighty man became weak. The man who took anything he set his eyes on lost his eyes. The man who menaced and terrorized Israel's enemies ground their grain at a millstone.

## BROKEN-DOWN WALLS

"A person without self-control," the wise man warned, "is like a city with broken-down walls" (Proverbs 25:28, NLT). When you let the walls around your life break down and go unguarded, devastating things can happen. It can end a marriage, ruin a career, cause a financial collapse, or destroy a ministry.

Of course, many have squandered their lives not so much in wrong actions but by taking no action at all. After long years of wasting their potential, they think, "Well, I don't guess I became everything I could have been had I shown more discipline. But things don't seem so bad."

Jesus told a parable about someone like that. In Matthew 25:14-30, he compared himself to a wealthy landowner who prepared to leave on a long trip. He called his servants together and handed them large sums of money. "See what you can do with this while I'm gone," he said. Upon the master's return, the faithful servants presented him with double the money he entrusted to them. But one said, "I didn't want to risk what you gave me in investments and business ventures: I buried what you gave me in a hole in the ground. Here you go."

Did the master say, "Well, at least you didn't lose it"? No, he said, "You wicked, lazy servant," and he cast him out of his presence.

If we squander all the talent, opportunities, and resources that God gives us, we might hear the same verdict upon Christ's return. Self-control isn't just about resisting poor actions; it's also about resisting lazy inaction.

## WAKE UP TO YOUR DESTINY

Thankfully, Samson's story isn't just about a mighty man ruined. Right after the writer told about Samson's capture and imprisonment, we get this quiet little verse: "But the hair of his head began to grow again after it had been shaved" (Judges 16:22, ESV).

The story isn't over after all!

Again, there wasn't anything magical about his hair. It was a symbol of a Nazirite vow that set him apart for God. So, his hair growing *back* alerts the reader that he had started to wake up to his destiny. As he trudged in a circle to push a Philistine millstone day after day, without the eyes that once led him astray, he ruminated on who he was supposed to be. It all began to grow back like his hair.

And one day, when three thousand Philistines were assembled during a great feast, they called for frail, blind Samson to be brought in to entertain them like a circus monkey. "Then Samson called to the Lord and said, 'O Lord God, please remember me and please strengthen me only this once, O God'" (Judges 16:28, ESV).

Samson got his hands on the two middle pillars on which whole structure rested, his right hand on the one and his left hand on the other. "Let me die with the Philistines," he prayed. His mighty strength returned to him, and he pushed the columns down, bringing the whole structure down on himself and the three thousand enemies assembled there.

It's a bittersweet ending to the story.

Throughout most of his life, he had wasted the mighty strength God had given him and failed to fulfill his destiny. It's only after he was reduced to a blind slave, with a heart broken by the only person he ever loved, that he called out to God for one more chance to get it right.

In this period of Old Testament history, God enlisted very imperfect leaders from among his very imperfect people to keep them from being exterminated by their enemies. So, the whole point of Samson's life was to preserve Israel from the threat of the Philistines. He finally accomplished that. As massive stones crushed the life out of his body, this blind, frail, and broken-hearted man finally aligned with his destiny.

*Don't wait so late to get things right, but get things right no matter how late it is*. "It ain't over till it's over," as baseball legend Yogi Berra once put it. So, call out to a gracious God.


## THE TRUE AND BETTER SAMSON

This story of how God used an *imperfect* man to save his people hints at another story of how God used a *perfect* man to save his people.

Jesus was the true and much better Samson.

- Samson's life began with a lengthy birth narrative, just like Jesus's story. An angel appeared to Samson's parents to announce the birth of one who would save God's people (Judges 13:5). An angel appeared to Jesus's parents to announce the birth of one meant to save God's people, too (Matthew 1:20-21).

- Samson's life ended with his arms stretched out to collapse the columns on either side of him, and in his dying, he saved his people (Judges 16:28). Jesus's life ended with his arms stretched out on a cross to save his people.

Of course, the difference between Samson and Jesus is found in all the years in between birth and death.

While Samson lived a dissolute life, frittering away his mighty strength, Jesus's life was very different. Jesus was "tempted in every way, just as we are—yet he did not sin" (Hebrews 4:15, NIV). He resisted all the things that Samson gave in to—and more. And so, when he died, it wasn't as a repentant failure like Samson. Instead, he died as the unblemished lamb of an Old Testament sacrifice. He died as our substitute to take away our sin so that we might be saved.

When you give yourself to him, he saves you, but he also starts molding you. He starts shaping you into the person he wants you to be, the person he is. He was one who "set his face to go to Jerusalem" (Luke 9:51, NIV) to fulfill his life's mission. So, set your face to live a life of resolution, too.

*"JESUS, I'M GRATEFUL THAT THE BIBLE STORIES ARE NOT JUST morality tales about how to live. The Bible stories are ultimately about you, not me. Samson's story is about you, not Samson. His story is about a God who calls and a God who resources us to fulfill the call —and his story is about a God who gives us chance after chance to come back after we've failed. Jesus, you are the true and much better Samson, who died to save your people, who died to save me. Save me. And each day, every day, I give you control so that I might have self-control. I want my longings and my judgements to be brought into alignment with you. Amen."*

# THE FRUIT OF OUR LABORS

*"Waste no more time arguing about what*
*a good man should be. Be one."*
Marcus Aurelius
*Roman Emperor and Stoic Philosopher*

N ow that we've explored the noble virtues that Paul called "the fruit of the Spirit," how do you feel about yourself?

I expect you're aligned with some of the nine characteristics, but you're struggling to master others.

In their study of the list, Megan Hill and Melissa Kruger wrote, "On good days, it's an encouraging list.... On bad days, it can be a crushing list—a testimony to how far you have yet to go. But the fruit of the Spirit isn't merely intended for self-examination. The list of fruit in Paul's epistle points us upward, away from ourselves, toward our Savior."*

This is what makes Paul's list of virtues better than any

---

* Megan Hill and Melissa Kruger, "Ten Things You Should Know About the

other list we could adopt as a pattern for life. Every other list is just another variation of demands that can only indict and not save. So many of our moral teachers are like lifeguards standing on shore and shouting to a drowning man, "Swim harder! Swim harder!"

But Paul's list of virtues leads us to Jesus, who provides the *pattern*, the *protection*, and the *power* we need.

**The Pattern We Need**. In this book, we've looked at remarkable men and women from the Bible who exemplified the characteristics we admire. But Jesus is our supreme example of every one of the virtues. That's really what the fruit of the Spirit is. It's a picture of someone who looks like Jesus. In his love, joy, peace, patience, kindness, goodness, faithfulness, gentleness, humility, and self-control, he "left you an example, so that you would follow in his steps" (1 Peter 2:21, GNT).

**The Protection We Need**. You're going to fall short of any list of virtues you aspire to. What then? The Bible warns us that these failures are evidence of our separation from God, and "*all* have sinned and fall short of the glory of God" (Romans 3:23, NIV). The very one who perfectly lived the virtuous life offered himself as if on an altar "like a lamb without blemish or defect" (1 Peter 1:19, NIV). His death on the cross was as our substitute, so that we may be saved. So, even as "all have sinned and fall short of the glory of God," the good news is that "*all* are justified freely by his grace through the redemption that came by Christ Jesus" (Romans 3:23-24, NIV).

**The Power We Need.** The message of the Bible is that the Spirit of Jesus lives within all who belong to him. So, Jesus

---

Fruit of the Spirit," *The Gospel Coalition*, May 14, 2024, https://www.thegospel coalition.org/article/10-things-fruit-spirit/, accessed 14 July 2025.

is not just an example to emulate. He is within us to encourage us toward greater maturity and to enable us to live in victory.

William Temple served as an influential church leader in the early twentieth century. He wrote:

> It's no good giving me a play like Hamlet or King Lear and telling me to write a play like that. Shakespeare could do it; I can't. And it is no good showing me a life like the life of Jesus and telling me to live a life like that. Jesus could do it; I can't. But if the genius of Shakespeare could come and live in me, then I could write plays like his. And if the Spirit of Jesus could come and live in me, then I could live a life like his. *

This does not mean that we have no role to play in pursuing the virtuous life. We have habits to change, websites to block, recovery meetings to attend, accountability partners to enlist, and all the other things that people do to improve. After all, Paul told us to "work out your own salvation with fear and trembling" (Philippians 2:12, CSB). Part of that consequential work involves personally developing the virtues.

And yet, right on the heels of advising us to vigorously strive to be better people, he wrote, "For it is God who is working in you both to will and to work according to his good purpose." (Philippians 2:13, CSB).

So, which is it? Do I become a better person through personal endeavor or because of God's sovereign direction?

Yes.

It's noteworthy that Paul called the virtues "fruit." Fruit is

---

* Quoted by John R.W. Stott in "The Model: Becoming More Like Christ," in The C.S. Lewis Institute, September 2, 2009, https://www.cslewisinstitute. org/resources/the-model-becoming-more-like-christ/, accessed 14 July 2025.

the final result of a process. After months of sunlight and rain and fertilizer and pruning, a tree bears fruit. In the same way, as you work out your salvation with fear and trembling while always confident that God is at work in your work, you'll find yourself becoming a virtuous person.

I've featured certain people from the Bible who exemplified the virtues, but—who knows?—it may be *your* life that someone highlights in a future book on the fruit of the Spirit.

Live to make it so!

# PLEASE LEAVE A REVIEW!

Help me get the word out about this book! Just one or two sentences from the online bookstore or review site of your choosing will make a big difference!

# ABOUT THE SERIES

The book you've been reading is part of a series of studies called *Bible Portals: Stepping into the Pages of Scripture*.

In the short books that make up this series, we'll look into passages like the Lord's Prayer, the Twenty-Third Psalm, the Beatitudes, the Armor of God, the Fruit of the Spirit, and others.

I call these *portals*.

Some of our favorite stories involve portals to other worlds or other eras. The characters step through the entry point on purpose or fall into it by accident. Either way, they discover a strange new world on the other side.

- Alice tumbles down the rabbit hole into Wonderland.

- Harry Potter discovers a whole new world on the other side of Platform 9¾ in London's King's Cross Station.

- An Iowa man hears a voice saying, "If you build it, they will come," and he constructs a baseball diamond in his cornfield that becomes a portal for baseball greats.

- Jack Skellington finds the Holiday Doors in the Hinterland and falls through one of them into Christmas Town, singing, "What's this? What's this?"

Eden Arielle Gordon explained why we love stories about mysterious entry points:

> Portals promise transcendence. They promise that there's something more, perhaps a grand design or some form of discernible meaning. We'd all love to know if there's something else out there in the starry night, as maybe that something would give us clarity as to why we're here on Earth at all.*

I've discovered some portals into the world of the Bible. Even if we've never read the Bible, we're familiar with certain passages. We quote them at funerals, print them on wedding programs, or recite them at recovery meetings.

Stand in proximity to these entry points for long and you may find yourself whisked into a place very different than your familiar life. It's a sprawling world of flawed heroes and sinister enemies, soaring poetry and pithy advice, prophetic warnings and hearty encouragement.

---

* Eden Arielle Gordon, "Portals to Other Worlds: Where Stonehenge, Harry Potter, and Dark Matter Meet," Magellan, 3 November 2019, https://tinyurl.com/2dm74oes, accessed 20 December 2023.

I hope you find your way into this world. As a Bible teacher for over forty years, I've seen profound changes in the lives of those who situate their little stories in the Big Story told in the Bible.

So, check out all the little books in the *Bible Portals* series. I'm hoping that these will serve as entry points for you into a lifetime love of the Bible.

A sample of another book in this series begins on the next page. To see the other books in this growing collection, go to the section of this book called "Also by Tom Goodman."

# EXCERPT FROM "THE LORD IS MY SHEPHERD"

*Here's a sample from the next book in the* **Bible Portals** *series. It's called* **The Lord is My Shepherd: Psalm 23 and Me**. *Get it wherever you buy your books online.*

David Diamond likes word tattoos. Whenever he sees one, he asks about it and posts a photo of the bearer on his Instagram.

Some are the names of loved ones. Others are inspirational quotes. Bible passages show up a lot.

In an article for *The Atlantic*, he reported that one biblical passage has been "a constant" in his photo collection.

Psalm 23.

Sometimes it's just the title inked on the skin. Sometimes it's a phrase from the poem. ("Fear no evil" is a favorite.) He's even met a few people who got the entire psalm etched on their skin in the original Hebrew language.*

The phrases of this little poem don't just show up on skin.

---

* David Diamond, "The Words People Write on Their Skin," *The Atlantic,*

The lines and images have impacted our culture's novels, films, and songs more than any other biblical passage.

Major composers like Bach, Bernstein, and Schubert have set the psalm to music. Queen Elizabeth wanted a seventeenth-century hymn version of it sung in her funeral service —just as she had it sung at her wedding.

Coolio opened his hit song "Gangsta's Paradise" by quoting from it. Megadeth recited the entire composition for the track, "Shadow of Deth," from their album, *The System Has Failed*. The Grateful Dead and Eminem have used some of the lines in their works, too.

You'll also find the verses in many films. *Full Metal Jacket. Titanic. We Were Soldiers. True Grit. Van Helsing. Terminator: Salvation.*

Louisa May Alcott alluded to the psalm in her novel *Little Women*. President George W. Bush recited part of the psalm when he addressed the nation after 9/11.

The poem's images aren't always employed in a positive light. In Pink Floyd's 1977 *Animals* album, the sheep of the psalm are derided as passive and easily led. In U2's song, "Love Rescue Me," the singer curses "thy rod and staff" because "they no longer comfort me." And Clint Eastwood's film, *Pale Rider*, opens with a girl reciting the entire psalm, stopping at the end of each line to complain about how God had failed to fulfill the promises. (Of course, since Eastwood's character mysteriously appears right after her prayer, the viewer can only conclude that God responded to all her troubles, after all.)

So, this little 3,000-year-old biblical poem has attracted

*https://www.theatlantic.com/ideas/archive/2024/08/photographer-word-tattoos/ 679511/*, accessed 8 May 2025.

widespread attention in our culture. But what do the words and images mean?

*Still waters.*

*The valley of the shadow of death.*

*My cup overflows.*

All the little books in the *Bible Portals* series are designed to bring readers into the world of the Bible by way of "portals." This is my word for biblical passages or images still familiar to people in our culture, even if they've never read the Bible.

Clearly, one of these portals is the Twenty-Third Psalm.

This poem encompasses all of life. Whether you're facing good days, bad days, or your last day, you'll find comfort and challenge in these six little verses. Let's explore the images and phrases that have captured the imagination of so many people across so many generations.

*Get your copy of* **The Lord is My Shepherd: Psalm 23 and Me** *wherever books are sold.*

# GROUP DISCUSSION GUIDE

## Coming Soon!

You'll soon be able to download a free copy of the Group Discussion Guide for all the books in the *Bible Portals* series.

To find out when this will be available, subscribe to Tom's devotional newsletter, *Winning Ways*. Find it at

tomgoodman.substack.com

# ABOUT THE AUTHOR

For over forty years Tom Goodman has discussed faith with believers and nonbelievers while serving as a pastor in Louisiana, the Cayman Islands, and Texas. He is a graduate of Baylor University and Southwestern Seminary in Texas, with a doctorate from New Orleans Seminary. He and his wife, Diane, have two adult sons. He enjoys scuba diving, fly fishing, and puttering around his woodworking shop.

**Subscribe to Tom's devotional newsletter, *Winning Ways*. Find it at tomgoodman.substack.com**

**f** X

# ALSO BY TOM GOODMAN

**Find these other Books in the "Bible Portals" Series**

**Book One:**

The Pursuit of Happiness: Learning from the Beatitudes

**Book Two:**

How to Talk to God: Praying the Lord's Prayer

**Book Three:**

Suit Up! Wearing the Armor of God

**Book Four:**

Nine Noble Virtues: Cultivating the Fruit of the Spirit

**Book Five:**

The Lord is My Shepherd: Psalm 23 and Me

**Other Nonfiction Titles by Tom Goodman**

The Anchor Course: Exploring Christianity Together

Repeat the Sounding Joy: The Four Christmas Carols of Luke's Gospel

Winning Ways: Inspiration for Uncommon Living

**Fiction by Thomas Goodman**

The Last Man: A Novel of the 1927 Santa Claus Bank Robbery

www.ingramcontent.com/pod-product-compliance
Lightning Source LLC
Chambersburg PA
CBHW060332050426
42449CB00011B/2737